CHRONICLES

OF
THE PAST GREAT RESET

ECHOES FROM A FORGOTTEN AGE:

Modern Pseudepigraphal Writings on the Past Millennial Reign of Christ, Satan's Short Season, and the War for Truth

Wild Remnant Publishing
Copyright © 2025

Wild Remnant Publishing
Contact at: wildremnantpublishing@gmail.com

© Copyright 2025

ISBN Paperback: 978-1-0688478-8-2

Table of Contents

Publisher's Introduction

A question has been haunting me in recent years: Beyond the Scriptures excluded from the biblical canon—those classified as apocrypha and pseudepigrapha—could there be other writings, largely unknown, that might have been considered sacred Scripture?

I have often discussed this topic with friends and colleagues. Are there still undiscovered texts buried beneath the earth, hidden like the Qumran scrolls? Could more Dead Sea Scrolls be waiting in some remote cave? And what about the Vatican's underground vaults—what long-forgotten knowledge has religious authorities concealed there? These questions linger in my mind.

Before continuing with this introduction, it is essential to define what is meant by apocryphal and pseudepigraphal writings.

Apocrypha – A collection of ancient writings, often of Hebraic or Christian origin, that are considered valuable but are not part of the official canon of Scripture in most traditions. Some are included in certain Bibles, like the Septuagint and

Catholic/Orthodox canons, but are excluded from the Hebrew Bible and Protestant Bibles.

Pseudepigrapha – A group of ancient religious texts written under false authorship, often attributed to biblical figures to lend them authority. These writings, typically from the intertestamental period, were never widely accepted as Scripture but provide historical and theological insights into Hebraic and early Christian thought.

I have an extensive collection of these works at home, and they have been a tremendous blessing to me. Not only do they contain profound wisdom, but they also, at times, illuminate our accepted Scriptures, bringing to light details that greatly enrich my understanding of God's Word.

The DaVinci Code Effect

Whether Christians like it or not, Dan Brown's *The Da Vinci Code*—both the book and the movie—reopened the discussion about the formation of the Scriptural Canon, which most Protestant scholars consider closed, meaning no more books will be added to the Bible. Nevertheless, Brown's work accomplished the following:

- **It Exposed the "Human Element" in Canon Formation** – The book highlighted the role of church leaders, councils, and politics in deciding which books were included, reminding readers that the canon wasn't divinely dropped from the heavens.

- **It Forced People to Reexamine Forgotten Texts** – By mentioning Gnostic gospels (e.g., *Gospel of Thomas, Gospel of Mary*), Brown made the public aware that early Christianity was more diverse than traditionally taught.

- **It Questioned the Authority of the Church in Canon Decisions** – It challenged the idea that the canon is purely "inspired" by showing how certain texts were rejected, sometimes for theological or political reasons.

- **It Made the Council of Nicaea a Talking Point** – Although inaccurately portrayed, the novel got people asking: *What really happened at Nicaea?* This led many to investigate the historical process of defining Christian doctrine.

- **It Revealed How History is Written by the Victors** – Brown's depiction of lost or suppressed writings made people wonder: *Were there valid Christian voices silenced?* Even if his version was flawed, it raised valid concerns about historical bias.

- **It Encouraged Skepticism Toward Institutional Religion** – Many readers came away questioning whether the Bible we have today was shaped more by power structures than by divine inspiration.

While scholars dismissed Brown's historical liberties, *The Da Vinci Code* nonetheless pushed people—both believers and skeptics—to rethink the formation of the both the Old and New Testament. It made them ask:

- *Why these books and not others?*

- *Did early Christian communities have different versions of the faith?*

- *How much did politics influence what we call "Scripture"?*

In short, while the book is not, in my opinion, historically reliable, it nonetheless sparked renewed interest in biblical history, leading many to study the real history of the canon for themselves. This, I believe, was much needed—and still is.

Are There Scriptures Being Written Today?

Another question that has been weighing on my mind is this: If believers today are indwelt by the same Holy Spirit as the saints of the past, could new Scriptures be written for our time by saints of today?

I know—it's a loaded question. Some might even call it sacrilegious. Besides, it's likely a moot point, as most scholars today would argue an emphatic *no* and dismiss the idea outright. Fair enough.

[...]

Yet, could this be one way in which we limit God? I am not asserting that additional Scriptures *do* exist—I am simply suggesting that they *could*.

After all, the Bible reminds us:

"If <u>the Spirit of him who raised Jesus from the dead dwells in you</u>, he who raised Christ Jesus from the dead will also give life to your mortal bodies through his Spirit <u>who dwells in you</u>." ~Romans 8:11, ESV

"Now there are varieties of gifts, but the same Spirit; and there are varieties of service, but the same Lord; and there are varieties of activities, but <u>it is the same God who empowers them all in everyone</u>. <u>To each is given the manifestation of the Spirit for the common good.</u> For to one is given through the Spirit the utterance of wisdom, and to another the utterance of knowledge according to the same Spirit, to another faith by the same Spirit, to another gifts of healing by the one Spirit, to another the working of miracles, to another prophecy, to another the ability to distinguish between spirits, to another various kinds of tongues, to another the interpretation of tongues. <u>All these are empowered by one and the same Spirit, who apportions to each one individually as he wills.</u> [...] For in one Spirit we were

all baptized into one body—Jews or Greeks, slaves or free—and <u>all were made to drink of one Spirit</u>." ~1 Corinthians 12:4-11 & 13, ESV

So, the conclusion one could reach in reading these passages is simply this: Since the same Spirit that resurrected Christ Jesus lives today in believers, and that same Spirit moved the apostles to write their gospels, letters, and epistles, could we not surmise that there is likewise a possibility of writings being written today by God's saints—who are also under the influence of that same Holy Ghost?

Controversial Writings

There are already books in circulation that claim to be inspired—some by God, others by different spirits. Many of these works present themselves as *new* scriptures or divine revelations, some of which have been around for quite some time. Some are as ancient as the Bible itself, while others are merely New Age philosophies disguised as sacred truth. The most notable ones are:

1. The Kolbrin Bible

The Kolbrin Bible is a collection of ancient writings that claim to preserve lost wisdom from past civilizations, including the Egyptians and Celts. It consists of two parts: The Egyptian Texts, said to be written by scribes after the Exodus, and The Celtic Texts, which allegedly contain wisdom passed down by early Britons. The book speaks of past cataclysms, moral teachings, and prophecies, particularly concerning a celestial body known as the "Destroyer" that may bring future disaster. While some claim it is an authentic ancient text, its true origins remain mysterious and highly debated.

2. Oahspe

Written in 1882 by John Ballou Newbrough, Oahspe: A New Bible is a spiritual text claimed to be received through automatic writing. It presents a complex cosmology, blending elements of Christianity, Theosophy, and Eastern mysticism. The book describes a vast spiritual hierarchy, the origins of human civilization, and a coming age of enlightenment. Oahspe promotes an egalitarian, vegetarian, and peace-oriented philosophy, rejecting traditional religious dogma in favor of divine revelations from angelic beings. Critics rightfully question its authenticity and source, while some view it as an inspired work of esoteric wisdom.

3. The Urantia Book

Published in 1955, The Urantia Book is a massive text claiming to be a revelation from celestial beings, providing a detailed cosmology, a history of the universe, and an expanded life story of Jesus. It introduces an elaborate spiritual framework, describing multiple levels of divine beings, planetary evolution, and the ultimate destiny of human souls. Many find its theological complexity intriguing, while others dismiss it as an elaborate hoax or pseudoscience. Despite its uncertain origins, The Urantia Book has influenced various spiritual movements and continues to have a devoted following.

4. A Course in Miracles

A Course in Miracles (ACIM) is a spiritual self-study book written in the 1970s by psychologist Helen Schucman, who claimed it was dictated to her by Jesus Christ. The book teaches a form of radical forgiveness, emphasizing that the physical world is an illusion and that true reality is only found in love and divine unity. ACIM combines Christian terminology with metaphysical and psychological insights, influencing New Age and spiritual self-help movements. While some view it as divinely inspired, others criticize it for diverging from biblical Christianity.

5. Conversations with God

Written by Neale Donald Walsch in the 1990s, Conversations with God presents a series of dialogues between Walsch and a being he identifies as "God." The book challenges traditional religious doctrines, promoting ideas such as spiritual self-determination, the illusion of sin, and a nonjudgmental God. It is written in a casual, conversational tone and has been embraced by those seeking a more personal and mystical relationship with the divine. Critics, particularly from Christian circles, reject its theology as unbiblical and human-centered.

6. The Archko Volume

The Archko Volume is a collection of supposed ancient manuscripts that claim to give firsthand accounts of Jesus' life, including letters from Roman and Jewish officials. It was originally published in the 19th century but was quickly accused of being a forgery. The book is filled with historical inaccuracies, anachronisms, and sources thought to be fabricated. Despite being discredited by so many, it still circulates among some groups seeking extra-biblical confirmation of Jesus' life. But most scholars consider it a hoax and an example of 19th-century pseudepigrapha.

7. The Kebra Nagast

The Kebra Nagast (translated as The Glory of Kings) is an Ethiopian sacred text that tells the legendary story of the Queen of Sheba, King Solomon, and the origins of the Ethiopian monarchy. It claims that Solomon and Sheba had a son, Menelik I, who later traveled to Jerusalem and brought the Ark of the Covenant back to Ethiopia. The text is foundational to Ethiopian Orthodox Christianity, linking the Ethiopian royal lineage to King David. While its historical accuracy is debated, it remains a revered work in Ethiopian tradition.

These texts, though vastly different in origin and theology, all claim some form of divine inspiration or hidden knowledge, appealing to those seeking alternative spiritual perspectives beyond traditional religious canons. I have read some of these—some more extensively than others—and, much like the pseudepigrapha, I cannot deny that they offer a measure of spiritual insight and knowledge for discerning biblical minds guided by the Holy Spirit. And there are others that I did not include here.

Hidden Millennium Knowledge?

One of the greatest mysteries I have pondered is the possibility that, during Christ's past millennial reign, many books may have been written by the saints who ruled the earth alongside Him. Could the apostles have composed additional works during that glorious time? A thousand years is a long span to go without writing anything, especially for those possessing great knowledge—which the resurrected and glorified apostles and saints certainly had in abundance. Furthermore, dare I ask... could the Lord Himself, as the supreme ruler and King, have written works during that era as well?

Consider, for instance, Solomon. I am convinced that he wrote many, many books, yet we are left with only a handful preserved in both Christian and esoteric traditions. After all, he himself declared:

"And further, by these, my son, be admonished: of making many books there is no end; and much study is a weariness of the flesh." ~Ecclesiastes 12:12

This strongly suggests that the renowned king was well acquainted with the writing of numerous books—many of which seem to have vanished from our reach. If such writings, whether from ancient biblical times or from what is now called the "Dark Ages," still exist, I firmly believe they are being kept from the general population. It would certainly serve the interests of the devil and his minions to suppress them during his "little season" of deception. Especially if what we call "the Dark Ages" was, in reality, the millennial reign of Christ, when *"the earth was filled with the knowledge of the glory of the Lord, as the waters cover the sea."* ~Habakkuk 2:14

Some have even suggested that the King James Bible, so beloved and revered, may not have been compiled under the authority of a 17th-century king but rather written by James the Apostle himself, during the millennial reign, when he ruled as a king over his assigned territory. If this were true, it would certainly help explain why this particular version of Scripture carries such an unparalleled weight of divine authority.

As further speculation, I have said it before, and I will say it again: we can only imagine the priceless writings, scrolls, and books hidden in the subterranean vaults beneath the Vatican—accessible only to those in power at the highest levels. I am certain that within those secret corridors, much truth is being withheld from the world. We would surely be astonished to find out what is truly being hidden there.

As a truther, I believe in seeking answers until I find them. And as the Lord Himself admonished, *"Seek, and ye shall find"* (Mt. 7:7). In the Gospel of Thomas, He pushes it further, saying: *"Let him who seeks continue seeking until he finds. When he finds, he will be amazed. And when he becomes amazed, he will rule. And once he has ruled, he will attain rest."*

Do New Revelations Require New Scripture?

We live in a time where knowledge and deception grow side by side. On one hand, we have never been more deceived than we are today—whether in religion, education, politics, or media, we are inundated with propaganda and falsehoods at an unprecedented scale. Yet, conversely, there has never been a time in human history when access to knowledge and information has been easier or more convenient.

With this growing knowledge, available to those who seek it, comes new revelation. After all, Jesus is no liar. He did say, *"Seek, and ye shall find"* (Mat. 7:7). And,

Solomon, the wisest of all men, wrote: *"It is the glory of God to conceal a thing: but the honour of kings is to search out a matter."* ~Proverbs 25:2, KJV

Just think—over the last quarter century, diligent seekers, many of them Christians, have discovered (or uncovered) the following:

1. The Deep Underground Military Bases (DUMBs) and Alien Deception

- Many missing children and human trafficking victims are believed to be taken into underground bases for dark experiments, hybrid programs, or food sources for non-human entities.
- The government's UFO/UAP disclosure is suspected to be a staged deception, prepping the world for a fake alien invasion (Project Blue Beam) or a "new savior" event.
- Some believe fallen angels and Nephilim hybrids are behind the UFO phenomenon rather than extraterrestrials.

2. The DNA-Tweaking Agenda (Vaccines, GMOs, and Transhumanism)

- Many believe that mRNA vaccines (such as those for COVID-19) are not just about immunity but a step toward genetic modification of humanity, potentially altering DNA permanently.

- GMO foods, synthetic meats, and nanotechnology in food and medicine are seen as tools for controlling human biology at a fundamental level.
- The Transhumanism agenda (merging man with machine) is believed to be pushed by elites like Klaus Schwab and the WEF, ultimately seeking to create a new kind of human, devoid of free will and easily controlled.

---

3. Worldwide Child Trafficking, Adrenochrome, and Elite Satanic Rituals

- The Epstein network only scratched the surface—global trafficking networks supply children for elite abuse, sacrifice, and adrenochrome harvesting (a chemical extracted from the adrenal glands of frightened victims, allegedly used for anti-aging and spiritual rituals).
- Hollywood, political elites, and secret societies (like the Freemasons and Bohemian Grove attendees) are often implicated in running these rings.

- Pizzagate, initially dismissed, has since been re-examined due to ongoing revelations about child trafficking at high levels.

---

4. The Mandela Effect: Evidence of Reality Manipulation

- A growing number of people believe our reality has been altered, pointing to changed historical events, altered Bible verses, and inconsistencies in memories that suggest quantum tampering.
- Some claim CERN's Large Hadron Collider has caused dimensional shifts, opening portals to parallel realities and subtly changing our timeline.
- This phenomenon has also been linked to simulation theory, where reality is being reprogrammed by an unseen force.

---

5. The Vatican and the Luciferian Control of Christianity

- The Vatican is believed to hide ancient knowledge, real Biblical texts, and prophetic truths while promoting a false, watered-down Christianity for the masses.

- The push for a one-world religion is part of the New World Order's Luciferian agenda.
- The third secret of Fatima is suspected to reveal the Vatican's collusion with Satanic forces to lead the world into deception.

6. The Flat Earth Theory & The Great Cosmological Deception

- NASA and other space agencies have deceived humanity for centuries about the true nature of our world.
- The idea that Earth is a globe orbiting the Sun in an infinite universe is seen as a Luciferian deception to hide the true geocentric, enclosed nature of our realm.
- Antarctica is actually the edge of the Earth, guarded by world governments to prevent exploration.
- NASA's moon landing and space travel are believed to be staged or manipulated to maintain the deception.

7. Mudfloods, Tartaria, and the Hidden Reset of Civilization

- Evidence of buried buildings and architectural anomalies suggests a massive reset event covered up by mainstream history.
- Tartaria, which is probably the vast and advanced civilization of the millennium of Christ, has been erased from history, along with its free energy technology and hidden knowledge.
- A great mudflood may have wiped out the old world, and survivors were reprogrammed through the orphan train system, World Fairs, and manufactured wars.

---

8. Satan's Little Season: The Hidden History of the Millennial Kingdom

- The belief that we are actually living in the period described in Revelation 20:3—where Satan has been "loosed for a little season" after a past Millennial Reign of Christ.
- This theory suggests history has been fabricated to erase the truth—that Christ's reign on Earth already happened, and we are now in the final deception phase before the Great White Throne judgment.

- Events like the Mudflood, Tartaria, and hidden resets suggest that entire civilizations and timelines have been covered up.

I could have listed more, but I believe these are the most notable conspiracies/discoveries that have shaken our world in the last quarter-century (2000-2025). This raises an important question: if such events had occurred in biblical times, wouldn't God have appointed a prophet, sage, or apostle to document them and expose the truth?

It also prompts us to consider additional questions, such as:

- Are there men of God *today* appointed to unveil these matters and write about them? Yes.

- Are they guided or indwelt by the same Spirit that inspired Christ Jesus and the apostles and prophets of old? Yes.

- Could their writings be regarded as holy or new Scriptures? No.

- If not, why not?

Playing Devil's Advocate

Here is another question to ponder: If new revelations were written in the style of the old King James Version (KJV), featuring pseudepigraphic authorship, chapter and verse format, and a careful commitment to

Scriptural truth and biblical alignment, how would believers receive them? Would they be automatically dismissed? Would they be categorized alongside traditional pseudepigrapha, albeit with a modern twist? Or, here's the kicker: if allowed to exist for a couple of hundred years, could these writings eventually be regarded as *a form of Scripture,* accurately portraying past events, exposing lies, and imparting wisdom?

That last point—*accurately portraying past events, exposing lies, and imparting wisdom*—is precisely what *Chronicles of the Past Reset* aims to achieve.

This book is written from the perspective of our current knowledge, taking into account the deceptions uncovered in recent years. Based on the high probability that we live in a post-reset world where Christ may have already returned, these modern epistles, letters, psalms, prophecies, and proverbs included herein are crafted to instruct and bless the modern reader with, if possible, new revelations and wisdom. Are these writings masquerading as Scripture? No. Nor should they be taken as such. They are, by all accounts, merely *pseudepigraphal* writings.

Written in an old King James English style, these works engage with beloved biblical narratives, reimagining aspects to harmonize with our contemporary reality. While they should not be considered Scripture and taken at face value, they offer valuable speculative insights and serve as a source of sound Christian wisdom. If, in reading them, you find yourself enriched and blessed, then one publisher can confidently say, "Mission accomplished."

And so, my hope, dear reader, is that you approach these writings with an open mind, just as you would any other pseudepigraphal works or high-quality Christian devotionals. May your life be enriched by their content and encouraged in your walk with God the Father and His Son, Jesus Christ.

Sincerely,

The Publisher

The Chronicles of Michael the Archangel

The Chronicles of Michael the Archangel is a pseudepigraphal work, the longest in this compilation, that recounts the momentous events that unfolded at the close of the millennial reign of Christ, following Satan's release, and leading into the beginnings of the past great reset. The writer, purported to be Michael, the Captain of the Lord's Host, reflects upon these pivotal events from his own celestial vantage point, offering a rare and profound perspective on the cosmic struggle between good and evil.

In chapters 3 and 4, the narrative delves into a masterfully reimagined dialogue between Michael and his ancient adversary, Satan, upon the latter's release from the abyss. This exchange, rich in theological depth, provides an enthralling exploration of angelology and demonology.

The later chapters provide a detailed and fascinating glimpse into the hidden history of mankind's forgotten past. They vividly depict how humanity fell under the dominion of Satan and his cohorts—

describing the mudflood, the lament of those left behind, the machinations of deception, and the gradual yet systematic rewriting of history. They further unveil how new generations were indoctrinated through orphanages, forced relocations, and incarcerations in insane asylums. The text also explores the role of infant incubators, the founding of the United States, the dark works of Freemasons and, ultimately, the future God has ordained to redeem mankind from evil once and for all.

Chapter 1

1 I, Michael, the chief prince and captain of the host of the Lord, make known the things which were, and which now are, and which shall come to pass.

2 For by the decree of the Most High, was the kingdom of Christ established upon the earth, and He did reign with power and great glory.

3 And with Him reigned His saints, those who had been faithful unto death; they sat as judges over the nations, and they taught the ways of righteousness.

4 For the resurrected ones, clothed in glory, did walk among the sons of men, instructing them in the law

of the Lord; and their word was as fire, and their wisdom was as a strong tower.

5 And the nations heard the word of the Lord, and many did submit, and they walked in the light of His counsel; but others turned away and served Him not.

6 And lo, the angels of God did labor with the saints, aiding them in their rule, in the building of cities, and in the ordering of all things upon the earth.

7 The work of men's hands was established in knowledge, for the Lord did grant them wisdom; and they built great habitations, and the cities of the world were filled with mighty works.

8 And the power of the firmament was given unto them, and the earth yielded strength, and no more was their labor in vain.

9 Yet the earth was not as the garden of Eden, neither was sin removed from the hearts of all; for though the Lord did reign, yet some did resist His dominion.

10 And there were houses and cities where the name of the Lord was not honored; and in their secret chambers did they plot rebellion, saying: 'We will not have this man to reign over us.'

11 And the Lord, who seeth all things, withheld the rain
   from their fields; and their land became barren,
   that they might know that He alone is God.

12 But they repented not; neither did they turn from
   their devices, but hardened their hearts all the
   more.

13 And the sin of those latter generations grew proud,
   for they were the sons of those who had not known
   the great tribulation, nor the judgments of God
   upon the wicked.

14 And though the saints reproved them, and the
   wisdom of the righteous was in their midst, yet did
   they love darkness rather than light.

15 For they said in their hearts, 'What need have we of
   the Lord? Who is He that we should serve Him?'

16 Thus, even in the days of the righteous reign, was
   the seed of rebellion planted in the hearts of men;
   and in the time appointed, it would bring forth its
   bitter fruit.

17 Now the thousand years drew toward their end, for
   the decree of the Father was unchanging, and all
   things must be fulfilled as it was written.

18 And thus do I, Michael, record these things, that the sons of the North, and all who seek the truth, might understand the times and the seasons appointed by the Lord.

Chapter 2

1 And it came to pass, when the thousand years of the reign of Christ were drawing to their end, the Lord did call forth a great assembly.

2 And all the resurrected saints were gathered together, those who had ruled in righteousness and judged the nations with wisdom; and the holy angels also stood before Him.

3 And lo, the throne of the King was set in the midst, and He who is called Faithful and True sat upon it, clothed in majesty and light.

4 And He lifted up His voice, and all the host of heaven and earth stood in silence before Him.

5 Then spake the Lord, saying: 'The time is fulfilled, and the hour hath come. The dominion given unto the Son by the decree of the Father shall now be withdrawn, and the things that were written shall come to pass.'

6 'Ye have reigned with Me, and ye have judged the earth in righteousness; ye have guided the nations and instructed them in My ways. But now, ye shall depart from these cities and go unto the place appointed for you.'

7 'For the earth must be tried once more, and the hearts of men must be revealed; and the adversary shall be loosed for a short season, to deceive those whose hearts incline toward evil.'

8 Then did the saints murmur among themselves, saying: 'Shall we depart from the habitations which we have built? Shall we leave the people whom we have taught?'

9 And the Lord answered them: 'It is the decree of the Father, and it cannot be changed. My Word is established from everlasting. Trust ye in Me, and lean not on your own understanding.'

10 And He bade them depart from their seats of rule, to take their journey unto a place prepared—a camp set apart, near the mount of the congregation, in the inmost parts of the North.

11 And they obeyed the voice of the Lord, though sorrow was in their hearts, for they knew that evil would again spread upon the earth.

12 And the angels also received their command, for the time of their open ministration unto men was now ended, and they ascended unto their stations above.

13 Then the Lord said: 'I shall dwell in the Holy City, even the Heavenly Jerusalem, and from thence shall I rule until the appointed end; and I shall go to and fro between the city and the camp of My saints at My pleasure.'

14 Then the Lord arose, and His glory shone forth as the sun in his strength; and the saints departed, as He had commanded them, and their cities were left empty.

15 And the people of the earth, beholding these things, were greatly troubled; and some mourned, for they knew that the light had departed from their midst.

16 But others rejoiced in secret, saying: 'Now is our chance; now shall we cast off His rule from us, and do according to our own desires.'

17 And the Lord beheld them, and He knew their thoughts; but He held His peace, for the time of testing was at hand.

Chapter 3

1 And the Lord sat upon His throne in the Holy City, and He called unto me, saying: 'Michael, Captain of the Lord's Host, stand forth.'

2 And I, Michael, hearing the voice of the Most High, did come before Him and bowed low, awaiting His command.

3 And the Lord spake unto me, saying: 'The hour is come. Go thou to the pit, and break the seal, and release Satan, that old serpent, which is the devil, and the adversary of all righteousness.'

4 And when I heard these words, my countenance was cast down, and sorrow filled my heart. For I am the guardian of Israel, the champion of the Lord's people, and the enemy of the accuser.

5 And I lifted up mine eyes unto the King, and I said: 'O Lord of Hosts, is there yet no other way? Must the deceiver of nations rise again to trouble the earth? Have not the people of the world known peace? Have they not dwelt in the light of Thy reign? Wilt Thou indeed permit the enemy to roam free once more?'

6 And the Lord, whose wisdom is beyond searching out, answered me and said: 'What is written must

be fulfilled. My Word is everlasting, and My decree changeth not. The hearts of men must be revealed, and all things that were spoken must come to pass.'

7 'Say no more, O Michael, for thou art My servant and My warrior; go now and do My bidding, for the time of trial is come.'

8 And when I heard this, I bowed my face to the ground, and I said: 'Thy will be done, O Lord Most High.'

9 Then I gathered my strength, and I took my sword and my shield, and I descended unto the pit where the dragon was bound. And as I came nigh unto the place, the earth trembled, and thick darkness arose to meet me.

10 For the abyss is a fearful place, a prison of shadows and chains, where the fallen ones are kept until the day of their judgment. And lo, the gates of brass stood before me, sealed with the seal of the Living God, even the same which I had placed there a thousand years before.

11 And I, Michael, did stretch forth my hand, and I touched the seal, and the light of the Lord departed from it. And the chains which held the dragon did shake and loosen.

12 Then I drew forth the key, given unto me by the Most High, and I placed it in the lock, and turned it. And there arose a great wailing from within, and the earth groaned beneath my feet.

13 And I beheld the gate as it did swing open, and a great and terrible wind burst forth, as of smoke from a furnace, darkening the sky above.

14 Then I stepped within, and the darkness swallowed me up. And I beheld a dreadful sight: the dragon, that ancient serpent, bound in the lowest depths, covered with chains of fire, his wings tattered, his form twisted, his eyes burning with malice.

15 And he lifted up his head, and his mouth curled in wicked delight, and he said unto me: 'At last! My time is come! Have the saints abandoned their cities? Have the rulers left their thrones? Hath the world been made ready for my hand?'

16 And I, Michael, answered and said: 'Thine hour is come, O adversary, but not for thy triumph. The Lord hath commanded, and I have loosed thee, yet woe unto the inhabitants of the earth, for great shall be their sorrow.'

17 Then Satan, that accuser of old, laughed a terrible laugh, and he said: 'Yea, thou hast loosed me, O prince of the Host, and for that, I thank thee. But

tell me, hath the world forgotten me? Do they still tremble at my name? Or hath the reign of thy King wiped all memory of me from the earth?'

18 And I answered him, saying: 'The world hath known peace and righteousness, and the name of the Lord hath been upon every tongue. But the hearts of men are foolish, and there are many who have murmured in secret, longing for rebellion. And the Lord hath decreed that thou shouldest rise, to deceive them that love not the truth.'

19 And Satan's eyes burned with cunning, and he said: 'Then my work shall be easy. For man, though he feareth God for a season, is ever drawn to iniquity. Yea, the flesh is weak, and pride shall be my snare.'

20 Then I, Michael, raised my sword, and I declared: 'Thy time is but a little season. Thou shalt go forth and deceive, but thy end is already written. The Lord shall consume thee with fire from heaven, and thou shalt be cast into the lake of fire forevermore.'

21 But the dragon only laughed and said: 'We shall see.'

22 And I turned from him, and the darkness trembled at my passing. And I ascended out of the pit, and I sealed it no more.

23 And the great dragon arose from the abyss, spreading his wings over the earth, and darkness followed after him. And he set forth to deceive the nations once more.

Chapter 4

1 And Satan lifted himself from the pit, and the blackness of the abyss clung to him as a garment. The earth trembled beneath his feet, and the air was heavy with the stench of his rising. And I, Michael, beheld him with loathing, yet I was commanded of the Lord to listen.

2 Then did the Adversary stretch forth his arms, and he laughed, for great was his delight in the freedom granted unto him. And he turned his eyes toward me, full of cunning and malice, and said:

3 "Michael, prince of Israel, thou hast loosed me at the word of thy Master. A thousand years have I lain bound in darkness, and my hatred hath been as a fire within me. But now am I unchained, and the fullness of my purpose shall be fulfilled."

4 And I answered him, "Thy time is short, O deceiver. Thou art loosed, yet only to thine own destruction. The Word of the Lord standeth sure, and He shall bring thee to naught."

5 But Satan sneered and said, "So thou dost believe. Yet I tell thee, the sons of men shall be mine, and their memory of the Just One shall fade as the mist of the morning.

6 "For in my chains have I devised a great and terrible work, a deception such as hath never been seen upon the earth. The righteous reign of thy Lord shall be but a whisper, a tale forgotten by fools. His laws shall I blot out; His times shall I make as dust upon the wind.

7 "I shall teach the nations to forget. I shall fill their minds with vain knowledge and empty wisdom. The chronicles of the holy shall be cast into the fire, and the words of the saints shall be counted as madness.

8 "For what is history but that which the rulers declare? And I shall raise up rulers in my image, who shall speak my words and walk in my ways. Yea, they shall rewrite the past, and the children of men shall believe it.

9 "The cities of the saints, the great works of the Millennium, shall I defile and cast down. I shall make them ruins and claim them as relics of an age long past, buried in mud and forgotten by time.

10 "And I shall raise up my own kingdom, and they shall call it new, yet it shall be founded upon the bones of the old.

11 "The wisdom of the righteous shall I make foolishness, and the foolish shall I call wise. The laws of God shall be cast aside, and new laws shall I give them—laws of deceit, disguised as righteous.

12 "Their children shall I claim, and they shall be taught my ways from their youth. They shall call good evil and evil good. They shall mock holiness and embrace sin.

13 "And I shall change the words upon their tongues, and the meanings of their speech shall I twist, that they may not understand the truth, even should they hear it.

14 "I shall raise up a great image in my likeness, and it shall be worshipped by all, whether they know it or not. They shall honor me in their new feasts and their festivals, in their symbols and their songs, and yet they shall not perceive that they bow before the Adversary.

15 "For I shall deceive them utterly. I shall give them knowledge, but it shall be false; I shall give them science, but it shall be vain; I shall give them progress, but it shall lead only to destruction.

16 "And the wise shall cry out, yet none shall hear them, for the ears of the people shall be dull, and their hearts shall be fat with lies. They shall love the darkness rather than the light.

17 "The kings of the earth shall I anoint, and they shall be my servants. They shall rule in my name and make war against the saints and innocent.

18 "And I shall give power unto sorcerers and enchanters, unto secret councils and men of craft, and they shall move the nations as a man moveth the pieces upon a board.

19 "Yea, I shall take the throne of the world, and they shall say, 'Who is like unto him? And who can make war with him?'

20 "And in the end, when all is fulfilled, when the nations are mine and the minds of men are darkened, then shall I finally ascend above the heights of the clouds. I shall sit upon the mount of the congregation, in the sides of the north.

21 "I shall be as the Most High."

22 And I, Michael, was wroth with a great wrath, and I lifted my hand against him and said, "Thou art a liar from the beginning, and thou shalt be a liar

unto the end. Thy works shall be brought low, and thy boasting shall be turned to wailing.

23 "The Lord rebuke thee, O serpent! The Lord rebuke thee forevermore!"

24 And I turned from him and departed, for my spirit burned with anger. And behind me, the voice of Satan yet echoed through the desolation, and the darkness gathered around him as a cloak.

25 And thus began the final deception of the nations.

Chapter 5

1 And when the Adversary was loosed from his prison, the whole earth shuddered at his rising, and the depths were broken up before him. And the Lord caused the very ground to convulse at the release of the dragon, that the wicked might be brought low and the haughty humbled.

2 And I, Michael, beheld as the fountains of the deep were rent asunder, and the earth did spew forth a flood—not of waters alone, as in the days of Noah, but a tide of thick mire, a deluge of clay and filth, which moved as a creeping plague upon the lands of men.

3 Lo, the mighty cities of the saints, which had stood in majesty under Christ's righteous rule, were cast down and swallowed. The great towers were buried; the palaces were choked with the dust of judgment.

4 And the people fled before the consuming tide, yet found no refuge, for the land was changed, and the works of their hands were entombed beneath the weight of the earth.

5 The righteous had departed, for the saints had been gathered unto the Lord, and their habitations stood empty, their halls silent. No longer did wisdom instruct the people, nor did the angels minister unto them.

6 And the wicked who remained were confounded, for their strength was vanity, and their wisdom was turned to foolishness. They cried aloud, "Where is the light of the world? Where is the knowledge that sustained us?" But none answered, for the days of righteousness were passed from them.

7 And those who had murmured against the King, who had withheld their worship and despised His commandments, were now without shelter. These had been judged even in the days of peace, for they had been deprived of rain in season, and their cities had languished.

8 Now were they left to wander as vagabonds, for their dwellings were no more, and their pride was brought to ruin.

9 Yet there were others—men of ancient rebellion, whose hearts had never known repentance, whose lips had cursed the Most High from generation to generation. These were they whom the Lord had cast out, that they should not defile the cities of the saints.

10 Through a thousand years had they roamed in desolation, like beasts outside the walls of holiness, unfit to partake in the kingdom of righteousness. They were wanderers, outcasts, a seed of defilement that awaited the rising of their prince.

11 And lo, when Satan was loosed, he went forth to seek them, to gather his own from among the scattered nations. He called them by name, and they knew his voice, for he was their father, and they had awaited him with longing.

12 With great rejoicing did they run unto him, saying, "At last, the chains are broken! He that judged us is gone! Our time is come!" And they fell down before him, and he embraced them, for they were his own.

13 Then spake the Adversary unto them, saying, "All these I will give you, for now the earth is mine.

Come, take dominion! Be princes and rulers in my kingdom! For as those called the saints once reigned, so shall ye reign in their stead!"

14 And they bowed before him, pledging themselves to his cause. These became the founders of cities, the builders of strongholds, the princes of deceit, the lords of men.

15 And Satan gave them wealth, and power, and knowledge darkened with iniquity. He taught them the craft of deception, the words that turn truth into lies, and the means to make themselves gods among men.

16 Then did the sons of perdition go forth, clothed in splendor and majesty, to deceive and to rule. And the earth, though still covered in ruin, was given into their hands.

17 And the remnant of mankind, those who knew not their right hand from their left, looked upon them and said, "These are our deliverers! These shall restore the world unto us!"

18 But they knew not that they were become captives, bound in the chains of the great deceiver, whose purpose was only to enslave and to destroy.

19 And so began the days of great delusion, the age of lies and of dark wisdom. For the truth, once shining as the sun in its strength, was now buried beneath the ruins, and the memory of righteousness was stolen from the sons of men.

20 But I, Michael, beheld all these things, and I knew that the Lord had not forgotten His own. For the end was written, and the hour of His vengeance was near.

21 For the Lord liveth, and He shall arise in fury, and the adversary shall be consumed in the fire of His wrath. His justice shall not tarry, nor shall His righteousness fail. Amen.

Chapter 6

1 This is the book of the generations of the great reset.

2 For the world had been overturned, and the foundations of all things were shaken, and a new age began—a time where truth was turned to falsehood, and the minds of men were darkened. And this was the beginning of the reign of those who had been born of the great deception, who knew not the ways of the righteous.

3 And in the midst of this reset, a new nation arose, known as the United States, a land of promise, a

land of freedom—yet one that had been secretly molded by the hands of the deceiver. The founders, though appearing noble in their eyes, were under the influence of dark powers, unbeknownst to the multitudes.

4 Among these founders was an image, a symbol given unto the people, a gift from the land of France. It was called the Statue of Liberty, a towering figure holding high a torch. But lo, in the depths of its creation, the truth was hidden. For this statue had been conceived not by the hands of righteous men, but by the dark occultists and Freemasons.

5 And this was no simple figure, no beacon of liberty as it appeared to the masses. For the light that it bore was not the light of truth, but the light of Lucifer, Satan's earliest angelic name. And the broken chains at the feet of the figure were not symbols of freedom, but of his past bondage in the abyss—a secret and subtle sign of the newfound freedom and coming dominion of the great deceiver.

6 Thus, the statue was set in place, and the people marveled at its beauty, its majesty, and its promise. Yet they saw not that they were being led into slavery, for they had been blinded by the light of false liberty. They called it a symbol of hope, yet it was the very mark of their bondage.

7 And as the years passed, the cities of the reset were occupied once more, but not by those who had known the truth, nor by those who had lived according to the righteous rule of Christ. Nay, they were overtaken by the deceivers, those whose hearts had longed for power and dominion.

8 Through deceit and lies, the people were once again placed in chains. They were taught false histories, and the memory of the righteous reign of Christ was erased from their minds. The truth became a relic of the past, forgotten in the flood of lies and corruption.

9 And those who had known the truth, those who had remained steadfast during the time of the reset, were no longer welcome in the new world. For they were a threat to the grand illusion that had been built. And so they were cast out—some were executed, others were placed in the asylums, where their minds were broken, and they were made to appear mad in the eyes of the new generation.

10 For the rulers of the new age knew that those who held the truth were the greatest threat to their reign. And so, with ruthless hands, they silenced them, made them appear as fools and madmen, that their voices might be stilled and their wisdom forgotten.

11 And the generations that followed were born into a world of lies. They knew not the truth, nor did they seek after it. Their minds were darkened, their eyes blinded to the reality that lay before them. The statues and monuments that had been erected in the great reset stood as constant reminders of their bondage.

12 Thus, the world was reformed, but it was not for the better. It was a world turned upside down, a world where darkness reigned, and the light of truth had been extinguished. And those who had once held the light now walked in shadow, their voices silenced, their names forgotten.

13 But I, Michael, do testify, and I bear witness to these things, for the truth shall not be hidden forever. The day cometh when the light shall break forth once again, and all that was concealed shall be revealed. And the kingdoms of the earth, which had risen in deception, shall be brought low, and the Most High shall reign forevermore.

Chapter 7

1 And I, Michael, do now recount the days that followed the great reset, when the children of the earth were born into a world that knew not the true righteousness of the Lord. For the parents of these children, who once had borne the light of truth in

their hearts, were now cast into asylums, their minds broken, their bodies made poor and destitute.

2 And lo, the children, those who had been born into this new age, were left as orphans—forsaken, abandoned, left to wander in a world that cared not for them. Their fathers and mothers, once the pillars of their homes, now lay in the chains of madness or were destitute, unable to support their young ones.

3 And I beheld the great world fairs that were held across the lands, fairs of wonder, as they were called. But these fairs were but a grand spectacle, a show of false hope, meant to distract the people from the truth. For within these fairs, there was a darker purpose, a purpose unknown to the masses.

4 In these fairs, infant incubators were displayed as marvels of science, but I knew their true nature. They were not used to nurture life in the way of the Creator, but rather, they were used for unclean purposes, to breed children by artificial means, to raise them without the warmth of a mother's love or the care of a father's hand.

5 These children, bred in such a manner, were not raised to be free, nor to be righteous, but to serve a greater purpose in the hands of the deceiver.

Possessing orphan spirits, they were taught to live according to the false narrative of the reset, a narrative devised by the dark ones, that they might be molded into servants of the prince of this world.

6 And in the orphanages, I saw the reprogramming of humanity at work—how the children were indoctrinated into the false ways of the world. The powers that be, the rulers of the new age, sought to rewrite the minds of the young, to sow the seeds of rebellion against the Most High, and to turn them away from the truth that had once been.

7 And the false teachings of Satan were spread throughout the lands, even as he had vowed to do when he spoke of his plans to me in the pit. The people were deceived, for they knew not the ways of righteousness, and they were made to believe in a new order, one that would serve the deceiver and his plans for dominion over all.

8 For the true faith of the Lord's way, once a light in the world, had now become but a shadow of its true self. The church had been corrupted, its teachings twisted and broken. The true faith had been obscured by false doctrines, and the people, though they called upon the name of the Lord, knew not the Lord in truth.

9 And this false religion, this counterfeit narrow way, became just like all the other religions of the earth—tools of control, instruments of bondage. The people were kept in chains, their minds and hearts bound to the teachings of men, rather than to the truth of the Word. And though they spoke of Christ, they knew not Christ, for they had forsaken His true ways.

10 Thus, the world was led astray, and the children grew up in a world where the truth was hidden, and the light of the Most High was but a faint glimmer in the distance. They were taught to follow after the ways of the world, to serve the powers that ruled over them, and to bow to the false gods of the age.

11 But I, Michael, do testify that the time is coming when all these things shall be made right. The truth shall be revealed, and the light of the Lord shall shine once again. And all those who have been led astray shall be called to account.

Chapter 8

1 These are the chronicles that I, Michael, have recorded, to bring truth to the godly remnant that remain in the final generation. For the days of deception are upon you, and many have been led astray. But these words, I tell you, are true and righteous, and they shall endure.

2 The Lord lives, and His promises are sure. His Word is faithful, and all that He has spoken shall come to pass. His making all things right is not far off. Behold, it is near—this time of restoration, of the setting things in order, shall not tarry. It is soon, and it will be swift.

3 But before that day comes, there shall be one final war—a war of great magnitude, one that will shake the earth and test the hearts of all who remain. It is the war of Gog and Magog, the final clash between the powers of good and evil. And lo, the enemy shall be as numerous as the sand of the sea, and they will rise up with all their might.

4 And in that day, the devil, Satan, that ancient Dragon, that old Serpent, shall lead them. He, who has deceived the nations since the dawn of time, shall gather his followers, the rebellious ones, from the four corners of the earth. They shall come together, in a great multitude, to make one last attempt to take over the earth and to dethrone the Lord of Hosts.

5 They will seek to take the camp of the saints, the holy ones who have been preserved and set apart by the Most High. They will come with fury, with hatred in their hearts, seeking to destroy all that is righteous. They will lay siege to the saints, seeking to bring

them into bondage and to force them into worship of the beast.

6 But fear not, O faithful ones, for Yahweh, our God, is with you. He has promised that He will not allow the enemy to prevail. Though the enemy come with their might, their numbers shall not stand against the power of the Almighty.

7 For just as the Lord has said, He will not be moved. He shall consume them all with fire from heaven, even as He has promised. The earth shall tremble, the skies shall roar, and the fire of His wrath shall descend upon the wicked. All those who have defied the Lord and sought to overthrow His kingdom shall be consumed in that fire.

8 And when the smoke clears, there shall be none left to oppose the throne of God. The enemy shall be no more, and the saints shall stand in victory, for the Lord, our King, shall reign forever and ever. His rule shall be unbroken, and His peace shall cover the earth as the waters cover the sea.

9 Therefore, be strong and take heart, O children of the Most High. For the end of evil is at hand, and the glory of the Lord shall be revealed. Hold fast to the truth, and stand firm in the faith, for your redemption draweth nigh.

10 Blessed be the name of the Lord, our God, the Creator of heaven and earth, the King of glory and the Lord of Hosts! To Him be all honor, and power, and majesty, both now and forevermore. His reign is everlasting, and His dominion is from generation to generation. Glory and praise be unto His name, for He alone is worthy of all worship. Amen, and amen!

The Lost Epistle of John the Apostle

---◆◆◆---

The Lost Epistle of John the Apostle is a thought-provoking text that invites the reader to contemplate a hidden chapter of history. Purportedly written at the close of Christ's millennial reign—sometime between 1075 and 1275—the epistle provides a striking continuation of John's exile on Patmos and the Lord's enigmatic words: "If I will that he tarry till I come, what is that to thee?" (John 21:22).

In this account, the apostle bears witness to the triumphant return of Christ, the establishment of His glorious kingdom, and the divine appointment of the resurrected saints to reign with Him for a thousand years. Chapters 2 and 3 paint a vivid portrait of life in the millennium, describing a world of beauty, justice, communion with angels, and harmony under the rule of the righteous.

Yet the heart of the epistle lies in its intended audience: "the chosen remnant of the scattered of Gog and Magog" (Ezekiel 38; Revelation 20). Addressed to those who would endure Satan's little season after the millennium has passed, it serves as both a testimony of the past and a prophetic revelation of truth in the midst of deception. Through exhortation and warning, the apostle calls this remnant to steadfastness, urging them to hold fast until the final consummation, when God shall make all things new.

Chapter 1

1. John, an elder and servant of the Lord Jesus Christ, whom mine eyes have seen, and mine hands have touched, the Word of Life, unto the chosen remnant of the scattered of Gog and Magog, who remain upon the earth in these last days, greeting.

2. I write unto you, beloved, that ye be not soon shaken in mind, nor troubled by the darkness of these times, for verily, the Lord reigneth still, and His Word shall not fail.

3. For ye have seen how the earth hath waxed old, and the righteous who once judged among you are taken from the earth, and the adversary is loosed for a short season.

4. Yet be ye not dismayed, neither let your hearts be troubled, for the Lord is faithful in all His ways, and He shall perform all that He hath spoken.

5. For behold, times and seasons are in His hand; He hath appointed the light and the darkness,

the planting and the harvest, the day of judgment and the day of restoration.

6. And this I testify unto you, that God is good, and all His works are righteous, though for a season the wicked seemeth to triumph.

7. Hold fast, therefore, and be steadfast, for the time of His final appearing draweth nigh.

Chapter 2

1. And I, John, bear record of these things, for the Lord appointed me to tarry till He came in His glory, even as it was spoken unto Simon Peter.

2. For I was upon the Isle called Patmos, exiled for the testimony of Jesus Christ, and I saw His day and rejoiced greatly.

3. And lo, He came upon the clouds of heaven, and the tribes of the earth did mourn, but the righteous rejoiced with exceeding great joy.

4. He brake in pieces the nations as a potter's vessel, and He reigned with a rod of iron; all things were put under His feet.

5. And I beheld the dead in Christ rise first, and I also was raised up, even I, who was the least among my brethren, and my flesh was made like unto the Lord's, incorruptible and full of might.

6. Then did He appoint unto me a portion in His kingdom, even ten cities did He give unto me to rule, for thus was it given unto the saints of the Most High.

7. And I walked among men, not as before, in frailty and weakness, but in strength and wisdom; and they did hearken unto the words of the Lord, and obeyed.

8. For in those days, righteousness and knowledge covered the earth, and the law of the Lord was the delight of the people, and peace was upon all nations.

Chapter 3

1. O what splendor was upon the earth in those days! For the cities were built in wisdom, and every work of men was wrought in holiness.

2. And the streets were paved with fine stone, and the habitations of men were adorned with gold and precious things, yet none did set their hearts upon them, for righteousness was their treasure.

3. And lo, the angels of God did walk among men, and did minister unto them; and the saints, who were raised in glory, did command them, and they obeyed.

4. And the children of men, who walked in obedience, did live many days, their strength not failing, neither their eyes growing dim.

5. For the knowledge of the Lord covered the earth, as the waters cover the sea, and the light of wisdom did shine in every dwelling.

6. And all who sought the Lord did find Him, and His presence was with them, and the days of men were full of joy.

Chapter 4

1. But now, O ye remnant, weep and mourn, for the time is at hand, and the end of these things draweth nigh.

2. For the Lord hath spoken, and His Word cannot be broken: Satan must be loosed for a little season, and the hearts of men shall be tried once more.

3. And in that day shall many depart from the truth, for they shall be given unto strong delusion, and shall believe many a lie.

4. The deceiver shall go forth among the nations, to deceive them once again, and to gather them together against the beloved city.

5. Behold, I tell you a mystery: they shall know not what they do, but shall be blinded by the rulers

of darkness, and shall rage against the saints, thinking to do well.

6. But I charge thee, O thou remnant of the faithful: Be not deceived! For the wicked shall surely perish, and they who trust in lies shall be consumed.

7. Stand ye fast, therefore, and let not your faith fail, for the Lord shall deliver His own.

Chapter 5

1. Yet be ye comforted, ye who tremble at His word, for the Lord is not slack concerning His promise, and He shall bring all things unto their perfect end.

2. For this short season shall pass away, and lo, He shall make all things new.

3. And the deceiver, even Satan, that old serpent, shall be cast into the lake of fire, and he shall be tormented day and night for ever and ever.

4. And the heavens shall be rolled up as a scroll, and a new heavens and a new earth shall be brought forth, wherein dwelleth righteousness.

5. And the throne of God and of the Lamb shall be in the midst thereof, and His servants shall serve Him, and they shall see His face.

6. And there shall be no more night, neither sorrow, nor crying, neither shall there be any more death, for the former things are passed away.

7. And the Spirit and the Bride say, come and be made manifest, O glorious will of the Father. And let him that heareth say, Amen.

8. As ye patiently await that day, may the will of the Father in heaven, the grace of our Lord Jesus Christ, the counsel of the Holy Ghost, and the communion of the saints be with you all. Amen.

THE BOOK OF THE PROPHET ZEPHANIEL

The Book of the Prophet Zephaniel is intriguing, to say the least. Beginning with the name of its pseudepigraphal author, which means "God has hidden" or "Hidden by God"—alternatively, "Treasured by God" or "God's secret." If this name were associated with an angel (as suggested by its "-el" ending), it could imply a celestial being entrusted with guarding divine mysteries. Indeed, some later mystical traditions mention an angel named Zephaniel in connection with hidden wisdom and sacred knowledge.

In this case, however, the author is human—and pseudepigraphal at that. Despite the name's Hebraic resonance, the text itself makes clear that its writer is a contemporary of our time, referencing both "media" and "pulpits" as evidence. Zephaniel is called to speak not only to "the children of the North" (North America) and "the nations of the earth" but also to the so-called lost tribes of Israel—particularly Ephraim and the "tribes of the north" (potentially Manasseh and Reuben in North America).

His message is a sobering one: That this generation has been deceived and is now living in Satan's little season—long after the millennial reign of Christ. The message is intended mostly for believers.

Like the prophets of old, Zephaniel laments to God about the stiff-necked and rebellious nature of His people, knowing they will likely not listen to His words. Though God confirms His unchanging decision to send him, the prophet is proven right—he is met with skepticism and scoffing. He rebukes their unbelief, alluding to the corrupting influence and ongoing deceptions of "those who say they are Jews, but do lie" (Rev. 2:9, 3:9). Nevertheless, God rewards Zephaniel's obedience with words of encouragement (Ch. 4:3-4), affirming his role as a watchman in these deceptive times.

Chapter 1: *The Call of Zephaniel*

1 The word of the Lord came unto Zephaniel, the
   servant of the Most High, saying:

2 "Arise, O prophet of the Most High, and speak unto
   the children of the land,
   Speak unto the sons of the north, and unto the

nations of the earth,
For I have a word against them, saith the Lord.

3 They have turned away from the truth,
And their hearts are hardened, for they are blind
to the times and seasons in which they dwell.
4 They know not that their day is waning,
And their hope is set upon the things of this world,
not knowing that the earth and its fullness are
mine."

5 And Zephaniel said, "Lord, how shall I speak unto
them?
For they are as the stiff-necked people of old,
And their ears are closed to the words of truth."

6 And the Lord said, "I will open thy mouth, and thou
shalt speak,
And I will send thee unto the lost sheep of the
house of Israel,
Unto the sons of Ephraim, and the tribes of the
north.
For I have called them, and they have forgotten
their first love.
Tell them of the truth of the past glory of the
millennium,
How my Anointed and beloved Son hath already
returned, and the tribulation is past,
And that they now live in Satan's little season."

Chapter 2: *The Rejection of Truth*

1 And Zephaniel rose early in the morning,
   And he went forth to the people, on every venue he
   found, speaking the word of the Lord,
   Saying: "Hearken unto me, O ye children of the
   earth,
   For the time of the Lord's return is not as ye
   suppose,
   For He hath already come and reigneth now,
   Though ye see it not with your eyes.

2 The thousand years of His reign have passed,
   And ye live now in the season of Satan's little
   while,
   A time when the enemy deceives the nations and
   blinds the minds of men."

3 And the people mocked him, and said,
   "What is this strange doctrine that thou speakest?
   For the Lord is yet to return, and the world will
   end in fire.
   We have heard it from our fathers,
   And we shall believe it no more."

4 And Zephaniel answered, "O ye foolish people,
   Ye see not the signs that are all around you,
   Ye trust in the lies of the world,
   And have made idols of your own desires and
   hopes."

5 "The Lord's return is not as you think,
    And the tribulation is a thing of the past.
    Yet ye do not understand, for your eyes are
    dimmed,
    And the rulers of this world have put a veil over
    you.
    They who say they are Jews, but do lie,
    Have woven a web of deception,
    And ye have become drunk with their wine."

Chapter 3: *The Conspiracy of Darkness*

1 Zephaniel spoke further, saying,
    "Behold, I have seen the powers of darkness that
    control the nations,
    Their webs are woven into the very fabric of your
    society,
    The conspiracies are everywhere, from the media
    to the pulpits,
    And ye have turned a blind eye to them.

2 Ye are ruled by those who serve the father of lies,
    Who deceive with smooth words and subtlety,
    Leading you further away from the truth.
    Yet ye say, 'How can this be?
    We live in a land of freedom and light, bathed in
    the Gospel.'

3 But I say unto you, your land is full of darkness,
    And the truth has been buried under the weight of

lies.
The rulers of this world have corrupted your
understanding,
And ye walk in the ways of Babylon, not knowing
that your heart is as the harlot.

4 They have made merchandise of your souls,
And ye know not that ye are being led to slaughter,
For the shepherds of this age have led you astray."

Chapter 4: *The Silence of the People*

1 Zephaniel lifted up his voice and cried,
"How long, O Lord, shall I cry out, and thou dost
not answer?
How long shall I speak to these people, and they
hearken not unto me?
I have told them the truth, but they are deaf to my
words.

2 Like those of old, they say, 'Where is the promise of
His coming?
For since the fathers fell asleep, all things continue
as they were.'
And I am weary of the mockers, and the scorners
who sit in the gate,
Whose hearts are full of deceit, and whose mouths
are full of lies."

3 And the Lord said unto Zephaniel, "Be not
dismayed,

For thou art not the first to speak the truth and be rejected.
They rejected the prophets of old, and they will reject thee also.
But thy words shall not return void,
And in the fullness of time, the truth shall be made manifest."

4 "For though they mock and scorn,
My people shall rise up,
And they shall see with eyes unclouded,
And they shall know the truth, and the truth shall set them free."

Chapter 5: *A Final Warning*

1 "Therefore, O sons of the north," saith the Lord,
"Return unto me with all your hearts,
For ye have strayed far from the ways of your fathers.

2 Ye have followed after the imaginations of your own hearts,
And ye have listened to the voices of the deceivers.
Repent, for the time of reckoning is at hand.

3 The hour is late, and the signs of the times are upon you.
Ye are surrounded by the works of darkness,
And yet ye have not wakened.

4 Turn back to the truth of the Word,
   For it is the only light that will guide you through
   the darkness.

5 I will give you the strength to stand,
   And I will gather you in the day of My wrath.
   But to those who persist in their unbelief,
   The day of judgment cometh swiftly,
   And who can stand in the day of My anger?"

Chapter 6: *The Prophecy Fulfilled*

1 And Zephaniel spoke again, saying:
   "Behold, the days are coming when the truth shall
   be known,
   And the deceivers shall be exposed.

2 The sons of the north shall awaken from their
   slumber,
   And they shall see the truth of the past
   millennium.
   They shall know that the tribulation is past,
   And that Satan's little season is upon them.

3 They shall no longer walk in the ways of darkness,
   But in the light of the truth.
   4 And I shall be with them in their battle,
   For they shall stand firm in the faith of their
   forefathers.

5 They shall fight the good fight, and they shall
    overcome,
    For the Lord their God is with them.”

6 “Thus saith the Lord: Let the one who has ears to
    hear, hear;
    And let the one who has eyes to see, see.
    For the day of reckoning is at hand.”

CONTEMPORARY PSALMS

Contemporary Psalms is a unique collection of twelve anonymous psalms, each offering a poignant reflection on the trials, triumphs, and truths surrounding the millennium, Satan's short season, the past great reset, as well as our current times.

Ranging from psalms of lament to psalms of resistance, from psalms of victory to psalms of rejoicing, these writings echo the cries of God's people across time—mourning the loss of the millennial kingdom, resisting the deception of the present age, proclaiming the certainty of divine justice, and rejoicing in the promise of final restoration.

Each psalm, in its own way, bridges past, present, and future—shedding light on the forgotten glories of Christ's reign, the harrowing reality of Satan's unleashed dominion, and the ultimate hope of God's people as they await His everlasting kingdom. Through these reflective verses, the reader gains deep insight into the struggles and perseverance of the remnant, offering both a solemn warning and an unshakable assurance of God's final victory.

Psalm 1: *A Cry for the Sons of the North*

1 O Lord, our God, who art high and lifted up,
　We, the Sons of the North, call upon Thee.

2 How long, O Lord, shall we wander in the ways of
　the wicked?
　How long shall we forsake Thy laws, and follow
　after the vain things of the earth?

3 The nations rage, and the people imagine a vain
　thing,
　But Thou, O God, art a refuge for Thy people.

4 Thou hast made the heavens and the earth,
　And Thy word is established forever.

5 Yet we have turned from Thy paths,
　And followed after the idols of the nations that
　came before us.

6 Shall we not return to Thee, O God, and forsake our
　iniquities?
　For Thy mercy is everlasting, and Thy grace is
　abundant.

7 Hear our cry, O Lord, and deliver us from the hand
　of the oppressor,
　For we have been cast down and our enemies have
　prevailed.

8 Yet we know, O God, that Thou art a strong tower,
   And in Thee we shall find refuge from the storm.

9 Deliver us from the deceivers who seek to destroy
   us,
   From those who say they are of Thy people, but lie.

10 Their falsehoods have darkened our
   understanding,
   But Thou, O Lord, hast revealed Thy truth to the
   humble.

11 Restore to us the years that the locusts have eaten,
   And let Thy light shine upon the land of our
   inheritance.

12 Let Thy people arise, and let the glory of the Lord
   be seen in the land of the North.

13 For Thou hast promised that in the last days,
   Thy people shall be gathered, and Thy kingdom
   shall come.

14 We wait for that day with expectation,
   For Thou hast shown us Thy mercy, and we trust
   in Thy salvation.

15 Lift up Thy voice, O God, and let the nations
   tremble,
   For the time of Thy judgment is near.

16 In that day, the enemies of Thy people shall be
   made a footstool for Thy feet,
   And Thy glory shall cover the earth as the waters
   cover the sea.

17 Therefore, we wait, O Lord, for Thy coming,
   And in the meantime, we will praise Thy name
   forever.

18 Blessed be the name of the Lord from this time
   forth and even forevermore.
   Let all the people say, Amen.

Psalm 2: *Psalm of the Desolate*

Composed After the Mudflood

1 O LORD, my God, I awake, and behold, the land is made desolate; the habitations of men are cast down, and the streets lie waste.

2 The city that was full of light is now a shadow of death; the houses are broken, and none dwell therein.

3 I cried unto Thee, but the heavens gave no answer; I looked round about me, yet there was none to comfort, for the righteous are fled, and the just are taken away.

4 The place of kings is become a heap, the throne of the mighty is cast to the mud. Where are the saints that once reigned in wisdom? Where are they that judged in righteousness?

5 Woe unto me! For I hearkened not in the day of mercy; I sought not the LORD in the time of His favor. The voice of wisdom called, yet I turned away; the gate stood open, yet I lingered in folly.

6 Now am I left as a sparrow upon the housetop, as a solitary dove among the ruins. My kinsmen are perished, my friends are cut off; my heart is faint within me.

7 The rivers run dry, the fields yield no fruit; the vineyards are laid waste, and the song of the reaper is no more. The beasts of the earth are fled, and the birds of the air have vanished.

8 O LORD, I am brought low; my soul is poured out like water. I wander as one stricken, my steps are weary, and there is none to guide me.

9 Yet will I trust in Thee, O Most High! Though I have been foolish, yet shall I lift mine eyes unto Thee.

10 Have mercy upon me, O God of my fathers! Hide not Thy face from the remnant of dust.

11 For Thy judgments are true, and Thy ways are just; Thou hast recompensed the earth according to its works.

12 But Thou, O LORD, art merciful; though Thou hast smitten, yet dost Thou heal; though Thou hast torn, yet dost Thou bind up.

13 O restore me, that I may walk in Thy statutes; revive me, that I may sing of Thy righteousness.

14 Yea, though the land be a wilderness, though the cities be fallen, yet will I hope in Thee.

15 For the Lord liveth forever, His mercy endureth to all generations.

Psalm 3: *A Lament Over Satan's Short Season*

1 O Lord, how long shall this wicked season endure?
How long shall the enemy have his reign of
darkness upon the earth?
2 The deceiver has gone forth with great fury,

And the hearts of Thy people are heavy with
blindness.

3 We see the storm clouds gathering, and the nations
    are in turmoil,
    Yet, O Lord, Thy people sleep, unaware of the
    times.

4 How long shall the sons of the North walk in the fog
    of deception,
    And the righteous stand silent in the face of evil?

5 Behold, the prince of this world is loose,
    His voices whispering lies to the ears of the
    unwise.

6 His armies march in silence, and the nations bow to
    his will,
    But, O Lord, where are Thy faithful who stand for
    truth?

7 The world is as a barren wilderness,
    And the seed of righteousness seems to have fallen
    upon stony ground.

8 Lord, Thou hast warned us of this time,
    When Satan would be loosed for a little while,
    And the hearts of men would fail for fear.

9 The rocks cry out, but Thy people do not hear.
The winds whisper the truth, yet they are deaf to
the call.

10 How I long for the days when we were a people of
light,
When our hearts burned with the knowledge of
Thy ways.

11 But now, O Lord, the darkness presses in,
And Thy people are scattered, as sheep without a
shepherd.

12 Oh that we would awaken to the hour at hand!
That we might return to Thee with all our hearts!

13 For the deceiver hath come, and the hour is short,
But we, Thy people, are caught in his snare.

14 We have walked the wide path, and now it is hard
to find the way back.
But Thy mercy, O Lord, is great; do not forsake us.

15 Open our eyes, that we may see the truth,
And give us hearts of courage to stand in this evil
day.

16 The hour cometh when the deceiver shall be cast
down,
When his lies shall no longer be heard upon the
earth.

17 But, O Lord, until that day, raise up a remnant,
A people who will stand for Thy truth, and declare
Thy justice.

18 Let us no longer slumber in ignorance,
But awaken to the times, and walk in the light of
Thy Word.

19 Blessed is the man who understands the times,
And walks in the knowledge of the Lord.

20 O that the hearts of Thy people would be stirred,
That they would no longer be deceived, but arise in
strength.

21 For the night is far spent, and the day is at hand,
Let us prepare our hearts for the coming of the
Lord.

22 Glory to Thee, O Lord, who hast given us the light
of truth.
Guide us, and strengthen us to stand in this
season.

23 We wait for Thy return, and for the day when all
things are made new.
Until then, keep us faithful, O Lord, and let not our
hearts fail.

24 Blessed be the name of the Lord forevermore.
Let all the people say, Amen.

Psalm 4: *A Psalm of Remembrance*

1 O my soul, remember the days of the King's great dominion, when righteousness covered the earth as the waters cover the sea.

2 In those days, the nations were at peace, and the cities of the righteous did shine with the light of wisdom. Justice and truth were established in the gates, and none did make afraid.

3 Year by year did the families of the earth make pilgrimage to Zion; from every land they ascended with joy to keep the feast of the Lord.

4 Though my heart was often heavy, though my feet were slow, yet did my father bid me come, saying, "We go up unto the house of the Lord, for it is meet to worship the King."

5 And lo, when I beheld the courts of the Lord, my spirit was lifted, and my lips did sing His praises.

6 The towers of the saints were as mountains of light, their halls were filled with wisdom, and from their mouths flowed knowledge like a river.

7 The bells of the sanctuaries did ring with healing, their tones restoring the bones of the weary, and their organs did send forth waves of life, renewing the flesh of the aged.

8 Yea, the fountains of the cities sprang forth with waters of life; whosoever did drink thereof was strengthened, and sickness found no place among the people.

9 The children of men waxed strong, their countenance as the sun; even the eldest among them walked with the strength of youth, for the Lord had set His hand to bless them.

10 No deceit was in the land, nor guile in the tongues of the rulers; wisdom was their portion, and the fear of the Lord was upon all.

11 In those days, the meek did inherit the earth, and the knowledge of the Lord did fill the land; the nations walked in His light, and His judgments were righteous altogether.

12 But woe unto them that turned away! Woe unto those who would not go up to worship the King! For the heavens were shut against them, and their land became as dust.

13 O my soul, how hast thou forsaken the days of thy youth? Why didst thou not hold fast to the fear of the Lord?

14 Yet even now will I remember His goodness; even now will I return unto Him. For the Lord changeth not, and His mercy endureth forever.

15 Let my heart be turned again unto Thee, O God! Let my lips declare Thy praise, and let my feet be swift to seek Thy ways.

16 For Thou art the same yesterday, today, and forever; Thy glory shall not depart, nor shall Thy kingdom be moved.

17 Blessed be the name of the Lord, who reigneth in holiness, whose wisdom is from everlasting. Amen.

Psalm 5: *Lament and Hope Renewed*

1 O Lord, how long wilt thou hide thy face from me?
How long shall I bear this burden, this weight
upon my soul?

2 For I have cried unto thee day and night,
yet my voice findeth no answer in the earth.

3 I walk in the midst of the scorn of men,
and they who see me mock and ridicule my words.

4 They call me deceived, they say I am an agent of darkness,
but I have spoken the truth, O Lord!

5 My soul is forsaken by all who once called me
    friend,
    for they cannot bear the truth I speak,
    and their hearts are hardened against thy words.

6 O how my heart is heavy within me,
    as though I walk alone in a desert of deceit.

7 They surround me with their lies,
    and I stand as a solitary witness to that which they
    refuse to see.

8 I am cast aside like the broken vessel,
    discarded by those I sought to help,
    abandoned in my hour of need.

9 And yet I cannot turn away,
    for thou, O Lord, hast opened mine eyes,
    and I am compelled to speak, though I stand alone.

10 The world lies in its sin,
    and I stand as a beacon in the darkened night.

11 My own house hath turned against me,
    my brethren call me a fool and a heretic.

12 O my God, where art thou in this hour of trial?
    Why hast thou forsaken me to bear such reproach?

13 Yet I know, O Lord, that thou art with me,
    even in the midst of my loneliness and disarray.

14 Thou hast promised to never leave nor forsake me,
   and thy Word is true, though I cannot see it now.

15 I shall trust in thee, O Lord, with all my heart,
   and lean not unto my own understanding.

16 Though the world rage and the wicked triumph,
   I will wait upon thee, for my hope is in thee alone.

17 My enemies shall not have the last word,
   for thy truth endureth forever.

18 I will sing of thy faithfulness in the night,
   and praise thy name in the morning light.

19 The burden is great, but thy grace is greater,
   and I shall find my rest in thee, O Lord.

20 For thou art my refuge and my strength,
   my shield in the day of trouble.

21 I will trust in thee, and in thee alone,
   for thou art my salvation, my God, my King.

22 Let the wicked say what they will,
   I shall not be moved,
   for the Lord is my rock and my fortress,
   and in Him will I place my hope forever.

Selah

Psalm 6: *Of Struggle... and Renewed Trust in the Lord*

1 O Lord, how long shall I suffer the venom of the
   wicked?
How long shall I be mocked and scorned by those
   who know not Thy ways?

2 My soul is weary with the insults,
and my heart is burdened with their relentless words.

3 They gather in the virtual streets,
and their tongues are sharp as swords,
they cast slanders and falsehoods against me,
but I have not forsaken Thy truth.

4 I walk in the valley of accusations,
my name is sullied by their deceitful lips,
yet I have not turned my face from Thee, O Lord.

5 They say all manner of evil against me,
but I have spoken Thy Word,
and it is the light that burns in the darkness.

6 They hurl their stones from behind their screens,
seeking to tear down my reputation,
yet I am not moved, for my hope is in Thee.

7 How long will Thou suffer their hatred to flourish?
How long shall I be a target for their mockery?

8 Their lies spread far and wide,
as they seek to drag my soul into the pit of despair.

9 O Lord, I am weary,
and my spirit is crushed beneath the weight of their
    scorn.

10 Yet, I will not give in,
for my heart is fixed upon Thee,
and I trust in Thy justice,
though the world may revile me.

11 They may scoff and spread their venom,
but I know, O Lord, that their end is near.

12 Thy truth shall prevail,
and they who have sown discord shall reap
    destruction.

13 Though the enemy surround me with their false
    accusations,
I will trust in Thy steadfast love,
for Thou art my refuge and my shield.

14 In the face of their attacks,
I will raise my voice to Thee,
for Thou art my defender and my vindicator.

15 When the wicked cast me down,
Thou wilt lift me up,
and when the storm rages,

Thou wilt calm the waves.

16 Let them slander me without cause,
let their falsehoods spread like fire,
but I will not fear,
for the Lord is my light and my salvation.

17 They may win the battle of words,
but the Lord shall win the war.

18 I will not cower in the face of their attacks,
nor will I bow to the idols of their scorn.

19 For Thou, O Lord, art my refuge,
my stronghold in the time of trouble.

20 I will trust in Thee,
and my heart will rejoice,
for though the world may rage,
Thy truth will stand forever.

21 O Lord, arise in my defense,
and let my enemies be scattered.

22 Let their mouths be silenced,
and let their lies be exposed.

23 I will trust in Thee,
and in the end, I will see Thy victory.

Selah

Psalm 7: *Psalm of Lament Over COVID, Its Vaccine, and Its Victims*

1. O Lord, my heart is heavy within me; mine eyes fail for weeping, for the children of men have been led astray.

2. The rulers of the earth have spoken lies in secret, and the nations have bowed before their words as an ox before the goad.

3. They have stretched forth their hands unto sorcery, and have trusted in the merchants of death.

4. Yea, they have taken into their flesh that which is unclean; they have defiled the temple of the Living God.

5. Behold, the blood of the innocent crieth from the ground; the streets are filled with the mourning of the bereaved.

6. The young and the old fall as sheaves before the reaper; the strong are cut down in the flower of their days.

7. Yet the people consider not; they see and understand not, for the veil of deception covereth their sight.

8. They are as sheep appointed for slaughter, for they perish for lack of knowledge.

9. Woe unto the physicians of deceit, and unto the kings who decree wickedness!

10. They say, "Peace, safety, and health," yet destruction cometh upon them unawares.

11. They trust in the works of their hands, and not in the Lord who giveth life.

12. They have forsaken the fountain of living waters, and have hewn out for themselves broken cisterns.

13. How long, O Lord, wilt Thou suffer the wicked to prosper? How long shall the deceivers go unpunished?

14. Arise, O God, and make bare Thine arm! Let the nations tremble at Thy rebuke!

15. Bring down the pride of the mighty, and let the counselors of iniquity be confounded.

16. For Thou art the Judge of all the earth, and the souls of men are in Thy hand.

17. Yet will I trust in Thee, O Lord my Redeemer; for the days of the wicked are numbered, and their end shall come suddenly.

18. The righteous shall lift up their heads, for their redemption draweth nigh.

19. They that fear Thee shall be as the cedars of Lebanon, unshaken in the storm.

20. And in the latter days, the knowledge of the Lord shall cover the earth, as the waters cover the sea.

21. Blessed be the name of the Lord, who maketh all things new! Yea, blessed be His name forever!

<hr>

Psalm 8: *A Psalm of Resistance*

1 O LORD, my Rock and my Fortress, the mighty have set themselves against me; the rulers of darkness conspire, and the kings of the earth take counsel together.

2 They say in their hearts, "We shall reign forever; our dominion shall not be overthrown." They forge chains for the sons of men, and with lying lips do they deceive the nations.

3 They call evil good and good evil; they turn judgment backward and cast truth to the ground. The oppressor waxeth fat in his vanity, and the sorcerers of Babel weave their spells upon the peoples.

4 But I shall not bow unto them, neither shall I accept their words; their doctrine is poison, their words are as vipers' venom.

5 They say unto me, "Trust in our wisdom, follow in our ways," but their wisdom is foolishness before Thee, O LORD, and their ways lead to the pit.

6 They seek to seal the heavens, to blot out Thy name from the earth; they would make of man a beast and of truth a lie.

7 But I set my face as a flint, my heart is steadfast in Thee; I shall not be moved, neither shall I fear the devices of the wicked.

8 The LORD is my light and my salvation; whom shall I fear? The LORD is the strength of my life; of whom shall I be afraid?

9 Though they decree unrighteous decrees, though they make the nations to drink of their cup of deceit, yet shall I not partake; for my portion is with the LORD, and my inheritance is with the righteous.

10 Yea, though they pursue me as the hunter pursueth the prey, yet will I trust in my God; He shall make

my feet as hinds' feet, He shall lift my soul above
their snares.

11 Their idols are vanity, their power but a shadow;
they are as grass before the whirlwind, as chaff
before the fire of the LORD.

12 The Almighty shall laugh at them; He shall bring
their counsels to naught. Their towers shall
crumble, their fortresses shall fall; the works of
their hands shall perish in the day of His wrath.

13 But the righteous shall stand; they shall not be
ashamed in the evil day. The remnant shall rejoice
in the LORD, and in His salvation shall they be
established forever.

14 Arise, O LORD! Let not the wicked prevail! Break
the arm of the oppressor, and bring forth judgment
upon the proud.

15 For Thy kingdom is an everlasting kingdom, and
Thy truth endureth from generation to generation.
Amen.

Psalm 9: *Hope and Joy Over the Awakened and Assembling Army*

1 Sing, O ye heavens, and rejoice, O earth!
   For the light hath shone upon the sons of the
   North,
   And the people who walked in darkness now
   behold the great light.

2 The hearts of the faithful are filled with gladness,
   For the truth has broken forth like the dawn,
   And the people rise from their slumber to give
   praise to the Most High.

3 Great is the joy of those who have been awakened,
   And in the gathering of the saints, there is
   rejoicing.

4 The Lord hath stirred the hearts of His people,
   And from the four corners of the earth, His army
   arises.

5 Who is this that cometh with great strength and
   power,
   Whose army marches in righteousness?
   It is the Lord of Hosts, mighty in battle,
   And His saints, who have been called, chosen, and
   faithful.

6 They stand in the truth of His Word,
    Their hands are cleansed, their hearts pure,
    And their voices are lifted high in praise and
    worship.

7 The army of the Lord is assembled,
    And they shall not be moved, for they are strong in
    His might.

8 The enemy shall not stand before them,
    For the Lord goes before them as a shield and a
    sword.

9 Rejoice, O ye people, for the time of victory is near!
    The final battle draws nigh, and the Lord shall
    reign supreme.

10 His enemies shall be consumed,
    The powers of darkness will fall, and the earth
    shall be made new.

11 The saints shall reign with Him forever,
    For they are the heirs of the Kingdom,
    And they shall inherit the renewed earth
    forevermore.

12 The sound of victory fills the heavens,
    And the earth resounds with the praises of the
    Redeemed.

13 The Lord hath brought His people into the light,
   And His truth shall shine forever.

14 O how blessed are those who have seen the truth,
   For their eyes are opened, and their hearts are
   filled with His peace.

15 They shall be counted among the faithful,
   And their names are written in the Lamb's Book of
   Life.

16 The armies of heaven and earth are gathered,
   And the final victory is certain, for the Lord is with
   us.

17 The battle may rage, but we stand firm,
   For our God is mighty to save, and His love
   endures forever.

18 The enemy's days are numbered,
   And soon, the Lord shall crush the serpent's head.

19 Let the redeemed of the Lord say so,
   Let the heavens declare His glory,
   For He is faithful, and His promises are sure.

20 Sing, O ye righteous, and shout for joy,
   For the Lord reigneth forevermore,
   And His Kingdom shall have no end.

21 Blessed be the Name of the Lord,
And let all creation join in His praise.

22 Glory, honor, and power be unto Him
Who sits upon the throne and unto the Lamb.

23 Let all the people say, Amen, and Amen.

Psalm 10: *A Psalm of Resistance*

1 The rulers of the earth speak great swelling words; they whisper among the nations, saying, "Come, let us rise up together, for a great evil is in the land."

2 They stir the hearts of the people with lying wonders; they declare, "The troublemakers must be removed, the enemies of peace cast down, for they stand in the way of our progress."

3 Yea, they call good evil and evil good; they make bitter for sweet and sweet for bitter. They fashion lies as armor and deceit as a shield.

4 The people, like sheep without understanding, hearken unto them; they run as a flood toward destruction, knowing not what they do.

5 They gather in council, saying, "Behold, the rebels! Behold, the enemies of the new way! Let us surround them, let us take their dwelling place, for they stand against us!"

6 But I shall not go with them; my soul shall not be joined unto their company.

7 Though they scorn me, though they mark me as an outcast, though they call me blind, I shall see the truth of the Lord.

8 Their words are smooth as oil, yet are they drawn swords; their banners declare peace, yet their hearts devise war.

9 Lo, the camp of the righteous is despised; they are afflicted and hated for the name of the Lord, yet their foundation standeth sure.

10 The multitudes know not what they do; they believe the sorceries of the wicked, and their ears are closed to wisdom.

11 Yet I shall not fear their threats, nor be swayed by their multitude. Though they press me on every side, yet will I stand.

12 For the Lord is my shield and my strong tower; He shall scatter the oppressors and confound the proud.

13 They think to uproot the holy ones, but the Lord shall laugh them to scorn; He shall arise in His might, and their mischief shall return upon their own heads.

14 The net they have spread shall ensnare their own feet; the pit they have dug shall swallow them whole.

15 I shall wait upon the Lord; I shall not take the hand of the wicked nor walk in their paths.

16 Though I be few among many, though I be reviled and cast down, yet shall my faith remain steadfast.

17 For the Lord my God reigneth; His truth shall not fail, and His judgment shall not tarry forever.

18 Blessed be the name of the Lord, who keepeth the righteous and bringeth the wicked to naught. Amen.

Psalm 11: *A Psalm of Rejoicing in the Lord's Majesty*

1 O sing unto the Lord a new song!
For though the heathen rage and the nations
   conspire,
Yet is He set upon His holy hill of Zion;
He reigneth in glory, unshaken from everlasting.

2 The sons of men say in their hearts, *Lo, He hath
   forsaken the earth!*
And the wicked boasteth, *Where is now thy God?*
But the heavens declare His dominion, And the
   firmament showeth forth His handiwork.

3 Behold! In the uttermost parts of the North, Where
   darkness sitteth in the season of the prince of this
   world, There doth the Lord send forth His
   witness—The lights of His majesty, the banners of
   His might.

4 The heavens are arrayed in colors most wondrous,
Emerald and sapphire, gold and crimson;
A pavilion of glory spread over the children of the
   North, That they may know and remember—He is
   near!

5 O ye righteous, be not dismayed!
For the Lord is enthroned in the sides of the North,

Even upon Mount Zion, where the foundations
  cannot be moved. The earth shall wax old as a
  garment, but His throne endureth forever.

6 Rejoice, ye saints of the Most High! Even now!
Sing praises unto Him with the voice of triumph!
For truth hath not perished from the earth, nor shall
  it be hid. The Lord upholdeth the faithful, and He
  shall arise in His time.

7 Glory and honor be unto Thee, O King of Zion!
Thy name is exalted in all the earth.
Thy light shineth in the darkness, and the darkness
  comprehendeth it not. Even so, avenge us quickly,
  O Lord our God!

Psalm 12: *A Psalm of Victory*

1 O sing unto the Lord a new song, for He hath
triumphed gloriously! The wicked rulers,
harbingers of past calamities, have fallen before
Him, consumed by the fire of His wrath.

2 The children of the great reset, who clung unto the
Lord, have been avenged; their foes turned to ashes,
their pride humbled in the dust.

3 The camp of the saints hath stood firm, and the hand of the Almighty hath defended them; no weapon that is formed against them shall prosper.

4 With a mighty shout, heaven hath opened, and the flames of judgment have rained down upon the adversaries; they are vanquished, cast into the abyss, never to rise again.

5 The tormentor of souls, the deceiver of nations, hath met his end; he is now tormented in the lake of fire and brimstone forever, unable to seduce or deceive the children of God.

6 Rejoice, O ye righteous, for the day of vengeance is upon us! The time hath come to claim the inheritance of the faithful, to enter into the joy of our Lord.

7 The voice of the Lord echoeth across the heavens, proclaiming, "Behold, I make all things new!" The former things are passed away, and the old earth and the old heavens have fled from His sight.

8 And there shall be no more death, neither sorrow nor crying; all tears shall be wiped away, and the former things shall be remembered no more.

9 For the Lamb who was slain reigneth in glory; He is the Light of the new Jerusalem, and His brightness doth illuminate the ages to come.

10 O blessed are they who wash their robes in the blood of the Lamb, for they shall have right to the tree of life and may enter in through the gates into the city.

11 In this new heaven and new earth, righteousness shall reign forever; justice and mercy shall kiss each other, and the peace of God shall envelop all creation.

12 Let every tongue confess that Jesus Christ is Lord; let every knee bow before Him, for He is the Alpha and Omega, the Beginning and the End.

13 O give thanks unto the Lord, for He is good; His mercy endureth forever. Let us rejoice and be glad, for our victory is assured!

14 The end is here, and the dawn of eternity hath come; forever shall we dwell in the glorious presence of our God, singing praises unto His name.

15 Amen and amen!

THE MUSINGS OF RICHARD, THE EARL OF SUFFOLK

Contemporary Wisdom for the Age of Deception

———··◆◆◆··———

*Set as modern wisdom literature with an ancient twist, **The Musings of Richard, Earl of Suffolk** is a pseudepigraphal work written in the style of Solomon's Proverbs or Ben Sira's Ecclesiasticus. With only one chapter, however, it is a much shorter composition. Its author is the enigmatic "Richard," who claims the title of Earl of Suffolk. The name Richard, meaning "rich and powerful ruler," hints that the author may be someone of financial means— though this remains mere conjecture. Furthermore, textual clues, such as references to technology and glowing screens, confirm that the author is a contemporary figure rather than one from antiquity.*

The book opens with a blessing for "the man who discerneth the times," a fitting introduction that aligns thematically with the other texts in this collection. The Musings offers sound wisdom for the present age, urging readers to place their trust and faith in God rather than in the wealth and influence of the powerful. It exhorts against the shedding of innocent blood and the love of money, echoing timeless biblical admonitions. Interestingly, the text's structure evolves as it progresses—shifting from a collection of reflective proverbs to an impassioned evangelistic plea, calling the reader toward spiritual truth and faith in Christ.

———·◆◆◆·———

1 Blessed is the man who discerneth the times, for his steps are ordered by wisdom and his path is secure.

2 Woe unto those who fill their minds with the fleeting news of this world; for they shall be led astray by the winds of doctrine that are not the Lord's.

3 The world speaketh of equality, yet they know not justice; they speak of peace, but they sow discord in their hearts.

4 The mind of man is consumed with devices, but few seek the wisdom of God through His Word, and thus they wander in darkness.

5 He that taketh pride in his own knowledge, without fear of the Lord, shall find that his wisdom is as a vapor before the Lord's understanding.

6 The media of this world speaketh smooth words, but their hearts are filled with deceit; trust not in their promises, for they are built upon lies.

7 He that trusts in the fleeting idols of this age, be it fame, fortune, or technology, is like a man who builds his house upon sand.

8 Life is not for the taking; it is a gift, a treasure to be protected. He that slays the innocent in his own hands shall meet with swift judgment.

9 They say there is no Creator, and they worship the creation, for they bow down to the image of man and beast. But the Lord made all things, and in Him alone is true glory.

10 Many call themselves wise, but their wisdom is as the grass of the field, soon withered. True wisdom cometh from God alone, and it is everlasting.

11 Do not be conformed to the patterns of this world; for the lust of the flesh, the lust of the eyes, and the pride of life are but a snare that leads unto death.

12 Woe unto them that shed innocent blood for the sake of convenience; they have defiled the land, and their hands are stained with iniquity.

13 The rulers of the earth conspire to deceive; they speak in dark riddles and cover the truth with their lies. But the truth shall find its way, for the Lord is its light.

14 Though they cry out for tolerance, they themselves are intolerant of those who speak the truth; they suppress the righteous and exalt the wicked.

15 Trust not in the promises of those who do evil, for their days are numbered. Their wealth and power shall fade away like a shadow at dawn.

16 A man is known by his words, but his deeds will reveal the truth of his heart. The wicked may speak of peace, but their actions are filled with strife.

17 The world hath set its heart on vanity, but those who seek the face of the Lord shall be found in peace, even in the midst of calamity.

18 The nations rage, and the people plot vain things. But the Lord reigneth, and He shall have the final say; all kings will bow before Him.

19 The youth are taught to follow their own hearts, but the heart is deceitful above all things; let them seek the wisdom of their fathers.

20 Woe unto the wicked who call good evil and evil good; they call for a new morality, but it is rooted in chaos. Righteousness shall be their undoing.

21 He that would be wise, let him guard his tongue; for the words of the fool are as a fire that consumes the house in which it is spoken.

22 There are those who cry for justice but know not the meaning of justice; they speak of rights but forget their duties. True justice comes from the Lord alone.

23 Do not place your trust in the systems of man, for they are corrupt and unstable. The Lord's kingdom is established forever, and His justice is perfect.

24 The wise man sees beyond the present, hearkening unto the warnings of the past; but the fool lives for the moment, blinded to the danger that approaches.

25 The love of money is the root of all evil; they that covet wealth shall be led astray into paths of unrighteousness and their souls will be lost.

26 Beware the digital idol, the false gods of this age. Many are ensnared by the glowing screens, but they know not that they are being led into captivity.

27 Keep thy heart pure, for from it proceedeth the issues of life. Let not hatred or bitterness find a home in thy soul, lest it defile all thy ways.

28 The world is full of distractions, and the noise of it doth drown out the voice of the Lord. Be still, and know that He is God.

29 The rulers of this age will not escape the judgment of the Lord. Their schemes are laid bare before Him, and their plans shall come to naught.

30 He that walketh with the wise shall grow wise; but he that walketh with fools shall come to destruction. Choose your companions with great care.

31 Woe unto those who forget their Maker, and turn their hearts to the vanity of this world. They shall reap the whirlwind, and their shame shall cover them.

32 In the last days, many shall fall away from the faith, deceived by the pleasures of the world and the deceitfulness of riches. Be ye steadfast, for your redemption draweth nigh.

33 The Lord is not slow to fulfill His promises, as some count slowness. His judgment is sure, and He shall make all things right in His time.

34 Fret not when the wicked prosper; they shall soon wither like the grass. But the righteous shall flourish like the palm tree.

35 The fear of the Lord is the beginning of wisdom; all those who hate knowledge and reject wisdom shall find their lives in ruin.

36 Trust not in man's understanding; seek ye the counsel of the Lord, for His ways are higher than our ways, and His thoughts, higher than our thoughts.

37 They say, "What is truth?" But truth is a Person, and His name is Jesus the Christ. He is the Way, the Truth, and the Life.

38 The kingdoms of this world shall pass away, but the kingdom of our God shall endure forever. Let us set our hearts on things above, where Christ is.

39 Ye have been called out of darkness into His marvelous light. Walk as children of the light, and let your good works glorify your Father in heaven.

40 The Lord will not forsake His people, nor will He leave them comfortless. Though the trials be many, He will deliver His own in the day of trouble.

THE CONFESSION OF BEELZEBUB

A Letter unto Asmodeus, Prince of Perdition

The Confession of Beelzebub is an unsettling and provocative text that presents a chilling perspective on the aftermath of Satan's release at the end of the millennium. This pseudepigraphal work takes the form of a private correspondence from Beelzebub to Asmodeus, that reveals the dark machinations of the fallen.

Beelzebub recounts the destruction of Christ's vacated kingdom, boasting of their success in corrupting mankind through orphanages, propaganda, and the transformation of sacred places. Yet, beneath his arrogance lies a growing fear: the human spirit, though broken, still hungers for what has been lost—even for truth. Memories of the past resist full extinction, stirring potential rebellion against the forces of darkness.

In a moment of treachery, Beelzebub questions his allegiance to Satan, who, according to him, is now unstable, guided by blind rage. He thus tempts Asmodeus with whispers of seizing power for themselves. This reflects the insatiable nature of evil—always grasping, never satisfied, and ultimately divided against itself—reminding us of the truth of Christ's words: "Every kingdom divided

---◆◆---

Chapter 1

1 Beelzebub, Lord of the Flies, First among the Fallen, sendeth greeting unto Asmodeus, Prince of Perdition, Corrupter of Kings, Master of the Hidden Arts. **2** Give ear unto my words, for the hour is dark, and the counsel of the Master is weighed in the balance.

3 Lo, since the chains of our Master were loosed, and since the fire of his torment was stayed for but a season, he hath sent forth his decree to subdue the earth. **4** The sons of men, frail and fickle, once knew the yoke of the Nazarene; for a thousand years were they ruled by His saints, and the cities of the world shone with the light of wisdom. **5** But now, the throne of the Just One is removed from their sight, and our dominion is come upon them.

6 Dost thou not remember, O Asmodeus, how the cities of the earth lay barren when first we gazed upon them? **7** Their streets were silent, their fountains ceased from their healing, and the temples of their infernal harmony were void of their accursed songs. **8** The habitations of the saints stood desolate, and lo, we rejoiced, for their kingdom had passed away. **9** A wasteland it was, and yet a land ready for the taking.

Chapter 2

1 Then did our Master send forth the decree: Erase, abolish, consume, and rebuild. **2** And thus did we conspire together to establish the new dominion upon the ashes of the old.

3 We spake, saying, Let all vestiges of the Nazarene's reign be stripped from the earth; let His name be known no more, nor His wisdom recalled. **4** His libraries have we burned, His monuments have we defaced, and His histories have we rewritten. **5** Let the orphaned children of His kingdom be gathered into our houses of reformation, that we may purge from their minds the knowledge of their fathers. **6** We shall raise them in our doctrines; they shall serve us without question. **7** Let the towering halls of their harmony be transformed into dens of revelry, houses of trade, and seats of our dominion. **8** That which once called the heavens to remembrance shall now serve our purpose. **9** Let great spectacles be devised, that the children of men shall believe a new history. **10** We shall give them wonders, pageants, and feigned marvels, that they may forget the past and adore the works of our hands. **11** Let the weak, the questioning, and the rebellious be marked, cast down, and broken. **12** Let them turn one against another, lest they remember the days of old and long for their return.

13 And thus was our decree established, and great was our haste to bring it to pass.

Chapter 3

1 Yet, O Prince, my heart is troubled, and my spirit is vexed within me. **2** The work is not yet as we had hoped, for the minds of men remember more than we expected. **3** Their spirits, though broken, yet hunger for that which they have lost. **4** They call it not by name, for we have taken from them the tongue of their fathers, yet still they seek, like blind men groping in the dark.

5 And lo, our Master is wroth. **6** His rage waxeth hot, yet he seeth not the errors of his design. **7** He speaketh madness, and his decrees become as sand shifting in the wind.

8 He saith, We shall enslave all! He saith, We shall silence every tongue! He saith, We shall erase every memory! **9** But I say unto thee, O Prince, the work is slower than he will admit, and his blind wrath shall be his undoing.

Chapter 4

1 Wherefore, consider now my words, and weigh them well. **2** If the Master faileth, if the dominion he hath sought crumbles beneath him, shall we not act? **3** Shall we not take the power into our own hands? **4** Together, O Asmodeus, we could rule. No more beneath him, but as Princes alike, co-heirs of the dominion that is now at hand.

5 Think on it, for the hour is coming when a choice must be made. **6** Meet with me in secret, and let us determine what is to be done. **7** But speak not of this to any but whom thou trustest, for even among us, eyes and ears abound.

8 The darkness is yet ours, but for how long?

9 I await thee.

10 Beelzebub, Lord of the Flies, First Among the Fallen.

The Epistle to
the Sons of the North

The Epistle to the Sons of the North *is an anonymous work. In that sense, it is reminiscent of the biblical epistle to the Hebrews. While the identity of its author remains a mystery, its intended audience is unmistakable: the "Sons of the North," a clear reference to the peoples of North America—specifically, the United States and Canada. This text serves as a poignant call to remembrance, urging North Americans to recognize their biblical heritage and encouraging a return to the faith of their forefathers and the God of Abraham, Isaac, and Jacob.*

Although directed at modern New Testament believers, the epistle is rich with Old Testament allusions, reinforcing the continuity of faith throughout biblical history. The author highlights the unsettling reality that we find ourselves in Satan's little season, expressing concern over the influx of immigrants and the resulting confusion of multiculturalism that has led to the worship of foreign gods.

In a heartfelt plea, the author exhorts readers to reclaim the faith that once fortified these nations, advocating for a return to the Word of God, a restoration of reason, and a prioritization of God, family, and country—in that order. The epistle concludes with a stark warning of impending trials, namely the coming battle of Gog and Magog, yet it also offers a message of hope: despite the chaos that may arise, God will ultimately save His people and restore all things.

Chapter 1: *Opening and Greetings*

1 To the Sons of the North, grace and peace be unto you from God our Father and the Lord Jesus Christ.

2 I write unto you, that ye might be stirred in your hearts and minds to return to the faith of your forefathers, and to consider the truth of your true identity.

3 For I see, as I look upon your land, that many of you have wandered far from the faith that was once given unto you.

4 Know ye not that your ancestors were the children of promise? And that through them, the promises of God have been made sure?

5 Ye are of the lineage of Ephraim and Manasseh, and even of Reuben. The tribes which were scattered are not lost, but ye have found yourselves in the land of your inheritance.

6 Therefore, let it be known unto you, that ye are not forgotten, but have been called to be a people of purpose, to walk in the faith of your fathers, and to return unto the God of Abraham, Isaac, and Jacob.

7 I speak unto you now, not as one who is wise, but as one who desires that you might return to the truth. For the time is short, and the enemy works tirelessly to deceive you.

Chapter 2: *The Season We Are In*

1 O Sons of the North, why do ye delay in seeing the times in which ye live?

2 For ye are not waiting for the return of the Lord as if it is far off; nay, ye are living in the season of the enemy's deception.

3 Ye dwell in the time when Satan has been given a season to work his wiles upon the earth, and the multitudes have been deceived by his devices.

4 But I call unto you, return ye to the words of our
  Lord and the apostles who walked with Him. For
  they spoke of their days as the last days, and they
  were as true in their day as in ours.

5 The time of which ye speak, that has been laid in
  your hearts, is not yet, for ye have been deceived
  by the rulers of darkness who have stolen your
  past and hidden the truth.

6 The buildings ye see around you, the great
  structures and monuments that stand as silent
  witnesses, testify that your forefathers walked with
  God, and that their work has been completed.

7 Remember the words of Jesus, who declared that if
  the people would not praise Him, the stones would
  cry out. And indeed, they have.

Chapter 3: *The Straying from the Word*

1 O ye Sons of the North, why have ye strayed from
  the truth of the Word of God?

2 Ye have given heed to the fables of men, and turned
  your ears to the voices that tell you lies.

3 But the Word of the Lord stands forever. Return ye
  to the teachings of the prophets, to the words of

Moses, the Psalms, and the holy apostles, for they
are your sure foundation.

4 And beware of the synagogue of Satan, for they who
say they are Jews but lie, seek to deceive the
nations and lead them into destruction.

5 The veil has been cast upon your eyes, but it shall
not last forever. The time of their judgment is
nigh.

6 Awaken O true Israel, for thou hast been deceived
by those who are not of thee. Return, return to the
Lord, and He will restore you.

7 The sword of judgment is at the door, and their
destruction is certain. The Word shall not fail, for
the promises of God are sure.

Chapter 4: *A Return to Reason*

1 O Sons of the North, ye have forsaken reason, and
have wandered after the desires of your flesh.

2 Ye have embraced the ways of the world, and
followed after the gods of the nations who came
into your gates.

3 The gates have been opened unto the barbarians,
and ye have mixed your seed with theirs.

4 But know this, that the ways of the Lord are higher than your ways, and His ways are for your good.

5 The desires of the flesh lead to destruction, but the ways of the Lord lead to life eternal.

6 Return, return unto the reason which God has given you, for He is the Creator of all things, and His wisdom is without end.

7 If ye walk in His ways, ye shall find peace, and your land shall be healed.

Chapter 5: *A Return to God, Family, Country*

1 O Sons of the North, I call unto you, return unto the Lord, and He shall heal your land.

2 For ye have turned away from Him, and in your wickedness, ye have been handed over to wicked rulers.

3 But if ye return to God, He will restore you. And ye must also return to your families, for they are the bedrock upon which your nation stands.

4 Train up your children in the ways of righteousness, and teach them to love the Lord their God.

5 Love your country, but let your love for God be first, for He is the One who has established it.

6 In these days, it is time to cleanse your hearts, and prepare your lives for the coming of the Lord yet again.

7 For if ye return to God with all your heart, He will heal your land, and your families will be preserved.

Chapter 6: *The Deception to Come*

1 O Sons of the North, beware! A mighty deception is nigh, and the world shall be greatly shaken.

2 The enemy shall gather the nations against the camp of the saints, and they shall seek to destroy all who are faithful.

3 But fear not, for the Lord shall deliver His people, as He promised. He will make your enemies a footstool for His feet.

4 And know this, the Gog and Magog war is at hand, and the forces of darkness shall gather to deceive all nations.

5 But do not be troubled, for the end is not yet. For the Lord's judgment will be swift, annihilating them with fire from heaven.

6 Therefore, prepare ye the way of the Lord, for the
   time is short, and the hour is at hand.

7 For in the end, the Lord will make all things new,
   and the light of His glory shall shine brighter than
   the sun forevermore.

8 Now unto Him who is able to keep you from falling,
   and to present you faultless before the presence of
   His glory with exceeding joy, to the only wise God
   our Savior, be glory and majesty, dominion and
   power, both now and ever. Amen.

THE EPISTLE OF JOHN-ETHAN

The Epistle of John-Ethan *offers an interesting perspective. While it stands as an epistle, it also reads like an apocalyptic text of old. Its unknown author, "John-Ethan," seems to hold a certain religious authority from his tone throughout. His name can be broken down into two components for its Hebraic etymology:*

1. ***John****: The name John is derived from the Hebrew name Yochanan (יוֹחָנָן), which means "Yahweh is gracious" or "God is gracious." The name combines "Yeho," referring to the divine name Yahweh, and "chanan," meaning to be gracious or to show favor.*

2. ***Ethan****: The name Ethan comes from the Hebrew name Eitan (אֵיתָן), which means "strong," "firm," or "enduring." It is often associated with strength and stability.*

Together, "John-Ethan" could be interpreted as "God is gracious and strong" or "Yahweh is gracious and enduring," combining the meanings of both names. He is the "son of Joseph, the Sidonian," which, strangely, may indicate the epistle was written in the

Middle East. The designation of "Sidonian" suggests a connection to the ancient city of Sidon, located in present-day Lebanon, known for its rich maritime trade and cultural exchanges during biblical times. Although the audience of the letter is clearly today's "North Americans," called the "Sons of the North," the provenance of the text seems to go way back, perhaps even to New Testament times.

This duality creates a compelling framework for the epistle's themes, which navigate the historical and spiritual landscapes of both past and present. John-Ethan's voice echoes the urgency of a prophetic call, awakening his audience to the profound implications of their biblical and spiritual heritage and the pressing need for repentance in a time marked by deception. As he lays bare the dangers that beset his readers, he offers not only a warning but also an invitation to return to the foundational truths of their faith. In doing so, he seeks to remind them that, despite the turmoil of their current age, the grace and strength of Yahweh remain steadfast, providing hope, guidance, and salvation for those willing to heed his words.

1 John-Ethan, son of Joseph, called the Sidonian, a servant of the Most High God, unto the children of the North, unto all the sons of the land of America, to those who are called by His name and yet slumber in the deceitful sleep of this age:

2 Grace, mercy, and peace be multiplied unto you, and a sound mind to see the times and seasons as they are. For verily, ye have not recognized the hour of your visitation.

3 Beloved, I sought to write unto you of the great salvation that we once knew, yet it is needful for me to remind you of the great peril in which ye stand, for ye have been beguiled. The Enemy, subtle and wise in his craft, hath led you astray with lies from the beginning.

4 The institutions of this age and the rulers of darkness have spread deceit to bind the hearts of men. They have masked the truth, hid the signs of the times, and given unto you a counterfeit hope. Ye walk in a delusion, unaware that ye are living in the season of Satan's rule.

5 Woe unto those who have received the lie as truth, for their eyes are veiled, and their hearts hardened. They mock the words of the prophets and heed not the cry of those who would warn them. Ye are drunk on the wine of the harlot's cup, and have forgotten

the call of your forefathers to return to the faith once delivered.

6 For ye are in the season when the great deceiver, the father of lies, hath been loosed for a time, and he hath beguiled the nations. His servants walk among you, cloaked in righteousness, yet they speak not the truth. These are they who have twisted the narrative of history, who have hidden the light of the truth, and who seek to keep you in ignorance of the signs of the times.

7 Ye have turned aside to fables and falsehoods, walking in paths that lead to destruction. Ye have sought the comforts of the world, and now the world hath become your snare. The ancient stones, which once cried out the truth, are ignored, and the cries of the faithful are silenced.

8 Yet there is hope, and the light still shines in the darkness. For those who have ears to hear and eyes to see, there remains a call. Return to the faith of your fathers, return to the Word of God that is true. Repent, ye sons and daughters of the North, for the time is short.

9 Behold, the day cometh when the deceiver shall be cast down, and all that is hidden shall be revealed. The lie shall be made manifest, and the truth shall stand as a pillar before all men. The great judgment

of God is at hand, and He shall make His enemies a footstool for His feet forever.

10 Yet even now, ye can turn to Him, ye can return to the path of righteousness, and He will cleanse you. He will open your eyes to see the deception that has held you captive. He will restore unto you the joy of His salvation, and ye shall walk in truth once more.

11 The time of the great separation is upon you. The saints of the Most High shall stand strong, and the enemies of God shall be consumed. He shall judge the earth one last time, and His Kingdom shall be established forever. The nations of the world shall bow before Him, and His glory shall fill the earth.

12 Let not your hearts be troubled, for He who is faithful and true shall triumph over all. Rejoice, ye who are awakened, for the vengeance of the Lord is near. The enemies of God shall be defeated, and the righteousness of God shall reign.

13 Even now, prepare your hearts, for the battle is before us. Stand firm, ye who are called, and see the salvation of our God. His victory is assured, and His Kingdom shall come, and His will be done on earth as it is in heaven.

14 Amen and Amen.

THE LETTER OF JOHN-ETHAN TO JUSTUS
John-Ethan, Son of Joseph, called the Sidonian, to Matthew, Called Justus, Son of Eleazar

The Letter of John-Ethan to Justus *is a personal letter reminiscent of those in the New Testament, such as Paul's letters to Timothy and Titus. Written by the same author as "The Epistle of John-Ethan," it seems to be addressed to John-Ethan's disciple, Matthew (commonly called Justus).*

The text suggests that the letter was likely written in a time of spiritual turmoil and deception, indicated by the warnings against false teachings and the call to stand firm in faith. While the specific time and location are not explicitly stated, the reference to Justus as a disciple and the overall tone of the letter imply that it may have been composed during the early days of the Church, possibly in a region influenced by both Hebraic and early Christian teachings, which could suggest a location in the Eastern Mediterranean or a similar context.

In this heartfelt correspondence, John-Ethan extends grace, mercy, and peace, emphasizing the importance of steadfastness in faith and the diligent practice of keeping God's Word before his household. He warns Justus of deceivers who distort reality and implores him to remain vigilant and rooted in Scripture.

John-Ethan encourages Justus to stand firm in his faith and to boldly proclaim the truth despite challenges—indicating that perhaps this was lacking. He reassures him of God's faithfulness and the ultimate triumph of light over darkness. The letter concludes with a personal touch, expressing a longing for fellowship and reinforcing their bond in the shared mission of faith. Ultimately, the letter, although written for a specific individual, offers keen reminders to today's believers to keep the faith, stand strong, and keep proclaiming the truth of the Gospel, especially in turbulent times.

◆◆◆◆

1 John-Ethan, a servant of the Most High God and of our Lord and King, who reigneth from the heavens, unto Matthew, called Justus, son of Eleazar, my beloved brother in the faith and fellow laborer in the truth: Grace, mercy, and peace be multiplied

unto thee from God our Father and the Lord Jesus Christ.

2 I thank my God always for thee, remembering thee in my prayers, for I have heard of thy steadfastness in the faith and thy diligence in keeping the Word of God before thine household. **3** Thou hast labored much in doctrine and in truth, not only for thyself but also for thy wife and thy children, that they should not be overtaken by the flood of lies which hath come upon the whole world.

4 My brother, see that thou remain unmoved, neither turned to the left hand nor to the right, but holding fast to that which hath been delivered unto thee. **5** For many deceivers have gone out into the world, speaking great swelling words, calling evil good and good evil, professing themselves to be wise, yet becoming fools. **6** They have led the people into delusion, saying, "Peace and prosperity," when there is no peace nor prosperity, and crying, "Trust in our rulers, the mighty of this world," though they be but blind guides.

7 Therefore, be thou diligent in the study of the Scriptures and in the continuous pursuit of wisdom, that thou be not taken unawares by the cunning devices of the enemy. **8** For Satan, as you well know, goeth about as a roaring lion, seeking whom he may devour, and his ministers appear as angels of light, clothed in the garments of righteousness, yet inwardly they are full of all corruption and deceit.

9 But thou, O man of God, continue in the things which thou hast learned, knowing from whom thou hast learned them. **10** Stand firm in the testimony of our Lord, who shall shortly put an end to the wickedness of this age, and bring forth the final judgment upon the kings of the earth and upon all that do iniquity. **11** Hold fast the profession of thy faith without wavering, for He is faithful that promised, and we know that our Redeemer liveth and shall reign forever and ever.

12 I rejoice greatly in thy boldness, my brother, yet I beseech thee, do not let thy heart be troubled by the fear of men, nor be thou dismayed at their scorn. **13** Speak the truth in love, with all boldness and eagerness, knowing that the Word of the Lord shall not return void. **14** For though the darkness is great, the Light of the world shall yet shine forth, and those who dwell in darkness shall see a great light.

15 My household greets thee, and we long to see thee soon, if the Lord permits, perhaps in the summer when travel is easier, that we may be refreshed together in fellowship. **16** Greet thy wife and thy children in the name of the Lord, and continue to shepherd them in righteousness and truth, as thou hast done.

17 Now unto Him who is able to keep thee from falling, and to present thee faultless before the throne of His glory with exceeding joy, to the only wise God our Savior, be glory and majesty, dominion and power, both now and forever. Amen.

APPENDIX I:

A MASONIC LETTER CONCERNING THE STATUE OF LIBERTY

Featured below is a speculative letter imagined to be penned by Frédéric Auguste Bartholdi, the renowned French sculptor behind the iconic Statue of Liberty and member of the Freemasons. This correspondence is directed to William A. Brodie, the Grand Master Mason of New York and the architect entrusted with laying the statue's foundation. The letter hints at the deeper symbolism and hidden meanings intertwined within this monumental work, suggesting that it represents more than just a symbol of freedom, but a manifestation of esoteric truths known only to those initiated into the mysteries of the craft.

Paris, France
January 12th, 1885

Worshipful Brother Brodie,

I trust this letter finds you in the best of health and spirits. It was a most enlightening occasion when last we met here in France, and I have since taken great care to incorporate into our endeavor the many details we discussed. The statue is progressing most favorably, and I enclose herewith several photographs for your review. The vision we share is taking form, standing as a beacon to the world, though only those with true sight shall perceive its deeper meaning.

As we spoke of during your visit, the composition follows, in inspiration, *Satan Summoning His Legions*—yet with a most fitting alteration. Rather than the dread solemnity of war's summons, we have chosen instead to depict the Master in his moment of triumph, offering his light unto the nations. The broken chains at his feet, subtle yet potent in their symbolism, declare the victory of his release but a decade past. His reign, long obscured, now resumes in the sight of all, though few shall recognize it for what it is.

You will note, too, that the figure bears an androgynous countenance, neither wholly masculine nor wholly feminine—a deliberate choice, as we agreed, to veil the deeper truths from those uninitiated. The public shall know only of 'Lady Liberty,' a radiant and noble form, yet those with understanding shall discern the greater mystery within.

I am most eager to hear how progress fares on your end. Have the foundation stones been laid according to the sacred measures we discussed? It is imperative that the appointed numbers and configurations be observed in full, for, as you know, such things are not mere ornament but necessity. I trust you have ensured that all is proceeding according to plan.

Lord Rothschild will, I am sure, be well pleased when I report to him upon my next visit to London. Should all continue as intended, our great gift shall be ready for shipment by the summer—perhaps as early as June. Arrangements for its passage across the sea are already well underway, and I anticipate no delays of significance.

I look forward to your reply and to the final stages of this most worthy endeavor. May the Great Architect continue to illumine our path.

Fraternally yours in Light and Truth,

F. A. Bartholdi

APPENDIX II:

An 1800s Letter from One Orphan to Another

Presented here is an imagined letter from a young boy named Thomas, addressed to his friend Joseph (or Joe), who has recently moved to Iowa. Set against the backdrop of New York City shortly after the unveiling of the Statue of Liberty, this correspondence reflects Thomas's struggles and disillusionment. As he recounts the festivities surrounding the statue's grand reveal, he grapples with feelings of isolation and questions the narratives of hope and freedom being propagated by society. The letter hints at a deeper, unsettling truth regarding the fate of orphans and the hidden realities behind the façade of prosperity, suggesting a conspiracy that connects their personal histories with the broader societal issues of their time.

New York City,
October 31st, 1886

Dear Joseph,

It feels like an age since you left. I reckon by now you've settled into your new life in Iowa, and I hope it's kinder to you than New York ever was to us. Do they treat you well? Do they call you son? Do you have a place at their table? I try to picture you there, far from the noise and filth, walking roads that ain't choked with soot, waking to the sound of birds instead of carriage wheels and the hollering of drunks. I wish I could see it. I wish I could have gone with you.

Two days past, they had a great celebration here. You should've seen it, Joe. Fireworks lit the sky, great bursts of gold and red over the harbor, and the people cheered like they'd gone mad. They say the whole world watched as they unveiled her—the great lady in the harbor, the Statue of Liberty. She stands taller than anything, torch in hand, like she's leading us all to some grand new age. The newspapers won't stop talking about her. The priests say she's a gift from God, and the politicians say she's a gift from France. But me, I ain't sure what to make of her. They say she welcomes the tired and poor, but I've yet to see the orphans fed or the beggars clothed.

I stood in that crowd, Joe, and I clapped with the rest, but all I could feel was how alone I was. I searched for you, even knowing you were gone, like maybe by some trick of fate you'd be there. But I was just another boy among a thousand faces, forgotten before the echoes faded.

I should tell you—I ain't at the home no more. I ran, same as we always talked about. You remember how they'd whip us if we spoke out of turn? Or lock us in the dark cellar if we fought back? I got sick of it, Joe. One night, I slipped out past the watchman and never looked back. I fell in with the newsboys, and now I sell papers on the street. It's no easy life, and I barely scrape enough to eat, but at least I answer to no one. At least when I lay down at night, there ain't no straps to hold me to the bed.

But Joe, there's something I can't shake. I don't know how to put it into words, but something about all of this don't sit right with me. The grown-ups talk like they got it all figured out, but I think they're lying—to themselves and to us. Ain't it strange, Joe, how many of us are orphans? Everywhere I turn, there's another boy with no mother, another girl with no father. And yet, there ain't near enough folk to have lost so many children. Why are there so few parents? Where have they all gone?

I keep thinking of my father. I was six when they took him, but I remember his face clear as day. He wasn't mad, Joe—not like they said. They called him "Crazy Jack" 'cause he kept talking about how the rulers hide the truth. What truth? What was he trying to tell me before they dragged him away?

I don't know, but I mean to find out. There's a boy in the newsboys' lodge, a sharp one named Eddie. He says he knows things—secret things—bad things. His ma was put in an asylum for no good reason, and he thinks there's more like her. Some of the older boys whisper the same. Maybe my father was taken to a place like that. Maybe your folks were, too. Maybe we ain't orphans at all.

Joe, ask your family again if they'll take me. I'll work hard, I promise. Anything would be better than this. But till I hear from you, I'm gonna ask more questions. I'm gonna find out what they don't want us to know.

Write soon, and don't forget me.

Your friend always,

Thomas

The Milan Cathedral—a sure remnant of past millennial glory.

The Chicago World Fair was just built different.

ALSO FROM WILD REMNANT PUBLISHING:

ARE WE LIVING IN SATAN'S LITTLE SEASON?

Exposing His Cunning Strategies to Deceive the Nations

"And he laid hold on the dragon, that old serpent, which is the Devil, and Satan, and bound him a thousand years [...], and after that he must be loosed a little season." ~Revelation 20:2-3

Ask yourself: Is it possible that the truth about the end times isn't what we've been told?

What if... the thousand-year reign of Christ in Revelation 20 has already happened? What if... Satan has already been loosed, and we are now living in his "little season"?

Are We Living in Satan's Little Season? © challenges conventional eschatology, exploring the unsettling possibility that Satan's release is not future, but a very present reality. Through scripture, history, and compelling evidence, this book uncovers forgotten truths and questions the world around us.

Through its pages, you'll take a deep dive into:

★ **Forgotten or Dismissed History**

★ **Misunderstood Scriptures and Eschatology**

★ **Unsettling Architectural Mysteries, and Much More!**

Could the lost civilization of Tartaria, dismissed as myth, be remnants of the Millennial Kingdom—a time of divine order erased by forces rewriting history? From mysterious architecture and suppressed technologies to the rise of global elites and mass deception, could the ultimate ploy be the concealment of Jesus's millennial reign and Satan's brief but powerful season of seduction?

Dare to uncover the mysteries of the past. Examine ancient clues, hidden technologies, and spiritual forces at work. Discover the profound implications of Satan's little season for today's deceived generation.

THE BOOK OF ENOCH

Large Print, Classic, Authorized, and Unabridged R.H Charles English Translation

The Most Revered, Essential, and Scholarly Translation of the Book of Enoch Available for Today's Most Scrutinizing Lay Readers, Students, and Scholars

The Book of First Enoch is a pseudepigraphal Hebrew apocalyptic religious text attributed by tradition to Enoch, Noah's great-grandfather, the seventh man from Adam. Offering a wealth of pre-diluvian and eschatological content, you'll find within its pages insights into the origins of demons and the Nephilim, an exploration of why certain angels (the Watchers) fell from heaven, a moral justification for the Genesis flood, much disclosure about our earth realm, and revelations about the Messiah's thousand-year reign.

Immerse yourself in the profound wisdom and prophecies of the First Book of Enoch with this 1917 authorized English translation by renowned Master of Ancient texts, Robert Henry (R.H.) Charles.

Featuring a thought-provoking introduction by Sebastien Richard; this unique version of the pseudepigraphal work will appeal to a wide spectrum of readers: beginners, seekers, readers of ancient texts, students, lovers of wisdom, scholars, and conspiracy researchers.

It includes these unique features:

★ **Large Print Edition:** This edition features an easy-on-the eyes 14-point type font, for added ease of reading and study.

★ **Unabridged Text:** Dive deep into the mystical world of Enoch with the complete classic English text of 1 Enoch as it was meant to be read by its ancient biblical author.

★ **Modern Chapter Numeration:** The chapter numeration was updated by replacing the translator's original Roman numerals with regular numbers. This makes for easy navigation for today's modern readers.

★ **Explanatory Chapter Subheads:** Navigate the depths of 1 Enoch with ease, thanks to carefully written explanatory chapter subheadings that provide invaluable introduction, context, and insights into the text.

Delve deep into the antediluvian world where angels, giants, and celestial realms intertwined with the human story. Unearth the timeless wisdom and hidden truths of Enoch in this unique edition. Embark on a faith journey through the ages, exploring the profound teachings and revelations of this highly esteemed extra-biblical text!

"The relevancy of The Book of Enoch at this time cannot be understated."

"Whether you're just curious, a student, or a scholar, this book will shock you."
"Enoch should be mandatory reading for all students of Bible prophecy."

The North Pole and Inner Earth Chronicles

Explore the Uncharted Depths of Earth's Mysteries in this Landmark Two-Book Compilation of The Smoky God and The Secret Diary of Admiral Richard E. Byrd

Uncover the secrets of the uncharted and delve into the enigmatic realms of inner Earth, beyond the North Pole, with this captivating compilation of two classic works about the hollow or inner Earth: ***The Smoky God: A Voyage to the Inner World*** by *Willis George Emerson* and ***The Secret Diary of Admiral Richard E. Byrd***.

The Smoky God: A Voyage to the Inner World takes you on a remarkable journey. Follow the adventures of Olaf Jansen as he recounts a mysterious voyage into the heart of our realm, through the North Pole, as recorded from his deathbed confession. Navigating the uncharted polar regions with his father, Jansen discovers a hidden civilization of giants and its awe-inspiring landscapes, captivating readers with vivid descriptions of an underground utopia.

The Secret Diary of Admiral Richard E. Byrd. This intriguing document chronicles Admiral Richard Evelyn Byrd's purported exploration of the Arctic's mysterious interior. Within its pages lies an account of a journey that challenges conventional beliefs about the shape of our Earth, provoking the imagination with its amazing tales of a hidden and highly advanced civilization residing past the boundaries of polar ice caps.

The North Pole and Inner Earth Chronicles © invites readers to indulge in these timeless explorations, sparking curiosity about the unknown and challenging established beliefs about our world. It is perfect for conspiracy researchers, adventurers, mystery enthusiasts, and for all those with a thirst for exploration and discovery.

This landmark edition also features:

- **Unabridged original accounts**

- **Pictures and maps**
- **A foreword by Sebastien Richard**

The Smoky God: A Voyage to the Inner World and **The Secret Diary of Admiral Richard E. Byrd** merge in this unique compilation to offer readers a captivating narrative that has fascinated generations.

Delight your mind's eye as you delve into these fascinating expeditions and accounts of the unknown depths of our earth realm.

ENJOYED THIS BOOK?

If so, please be kind and leave a review on: